JUMP Math 5.2
Book 5 Part 2 of 2

Contents

jump math™

MULTIPLYING POTENTIAL.

JUMP Math
One Yonge Street, Suite 1014
Toronto, Ontario M5E 1E5
Canada
www.jumpmath.org

Writers: Dr. Francisco Kibedi, Julie Lorinc, Dr. Sohrab Rahbar
Editors: Megan Burns, Liane Tsui, Natalie Francis, Lindsay Karpenko, Holly Dickinson, Jodi Rauch
Layout and Illustrations: Linh Lam, Sawyer Paul, Klaudia Bednarczyk
Cover Design: Sawyer Paul, based on original design by Blakeley Words+Pictures (2014)
Cover Photograph: © Vito DeFilippo/Shutterstock

ISBN 978-1-77395-049-5

Fourth printing June 2022

Printed and bound in Canada

Welcome to JUMP Math

Entering the world of JUMP Math means believing that every child has the capacity to be fully numerate and to love math. Founder and mathematician John Mighton has used this premise to develop his innovative teaching method. The resulting resources isolate and describe concepts so clearly and incrementally that everyone can understand them.

JUMP Math is comprised of Teacher Resources, Digital Lesson Slides, student Assessment & Practice Books, assessment tools, outreach programs, and professional development. All of this is presented on the JUMP Math website: **www.jumpmath.org**.

The Teacher Resource is available on the website for free use. Read the introduction to the Teacher Resource before you begin using these materials. This will ensure that you understand both the philosophy and the methodology of JUMP Math. The Assessment & Practice Books are designed for use by students, with adult guidance. Each student will have unique needs and it is important to provide the student with the appropriate support and encouragement as they work through the material.

Allow students to discover the concepts by themselves as much as possible. Mathematical discoveries can be made in small, incremental steps. The discovery of a new step is like untangling the parts of a puzzle. It is exciting and rewarding.

Students will need to answer the questions marked with a ▤ in a notebook. Grid paper notebooks should always be on hand for answering extra questions or when additional room for calculation is needed.

Contents

Unit 4: Number Sense: Dividing Whole Numbers

Unit 5: Measurement: Length and Time

Unit 6: Geometry: Angles and Polygons

Unit 7: Probability and Data Management: Graphs and Surveys

PART 2
Unit 8: Patterns and Algebra: Variables, Expressions, and Equations

Unit 9: Number Sense: Fractions

Unit 10: Number Sense: Decimals

Unit 11: Number Sense: Using Decimals

Unit 12: Geometry: Coordinates and Transformations

Unit 13: Geometry: 3-D Shapes

Unit 14: Measurement: Perimeter, Area, Volume, and Mass

Unit 15: Probability and Data Management: Likelihood and Probability

PA5-8 Numerical Expressions

A **numerical expression** is a combination of numbers, operation signs, and sometimes brackets that represents a quantity.

Example: These numerical expressions all represent 10.

$5 + 2 + 3$ $\qquad$ $14 - 4$ $\qquad$ $70 \div 7$ $\qquad$ $(3 + 2) \times 2$

1. Calculate the numerical expression.

a) $2 + 5 + 1$ _____

b) 2×5 _____

c) $3 \times 2 \times 4$ _____

d) $(8 \times 3) \div 2$ _____

e) $(1 + 3) \times 4$ _____

f) $3 + (6 \div 2)$ _____

g) $(6 \times 3) \div 2$ _____

h) $(10 - 4) \div 2$ _____

i) $10 - (4 \div 2)$ _____

2. Write the number 3 in the box and then calculate the expression.

a) $\boxed{3} + 4 \longrightarrow \underline{\ 7\ }$

b) $\boxed{3} + 2 \longrightarrow$ _____

c) $9 - \boxed{} \longrightarrow$ _____

d) $\boxed{} - 2 \longrightarrow$ _____

e) $\boxed{} \times 5 \longrightarrow$ _____

f) $18 \div \boxed{} \longrightarrow$ _____

An **equation** is a statement that has two equal expressions separated by an equal sign.

Examples: $14 - 4 = 70 \div 7$ $\qquad$ $12 = 3 \times 4$

3. a) Circle two expressions in Question 1 that represent the same number.

 b) Write an equation using the two expressions.

 _____ = _____

4. Verify that the equation is true.

a) $(4 + 3) \times 2 = (5 \times 3) - 1$

 $(4 + 3) \times 2$ and $(5 \times 3) - 1$

 $= 7 \times 2 \qquad\qquad = 15 - 1$

 $= 14 \qquad\qquad\quad = 14$

b) $2 \times 4 \times 5 = 4 \times 10$

 $2 \times 4 \times 5$ and 4×10

c) $3 + 11 = (3 + 1) + (11 - 1)$

 $3 + 11$ and $(3 + 1) + (11 - 1)$

d) $3 + 11 = (3 + 2) + (11 - 2)$

 $3 + 11$ and $(3 + 2) + (11 - 2)$

PA5-9 Unknown Quantities and Equations

1. Some apples are inside a bag and some are outside the bag. The total number of apples is shown. Draw the missing apples in the bag.

   a)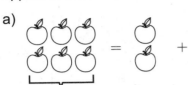

   total number of apples

   b)

   c)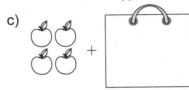

   d)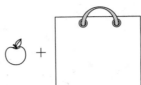

2. Draw the missing apples in the bag. Then write an equation (with numbers) to represent the picture.

   a)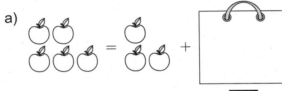

   _5_ = _3_ + ☐

   b)

   ____ = ____ + ☐

   c)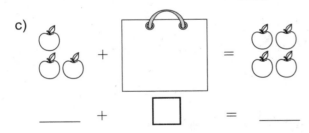

   ____ + ☐ = ____

   d)

   ____ + ☐ = ____

3. Write an equation for each problem. Use a box for the unknown quantity.

   a) There are 7 apples altogether. There are 4 outside a basket. How many are inside?

   _7_ = _4_ + ☐

   b) There are 9 apples altogether. There are 7 outside a basket. How many are inside?

   ____ = ____ + ☐

   c) There are 11 plums altogether. There are 5 inside a bag. How many are outside?

   d) 17 students are at the library. There are 9 in the computer room. How many are outside the computer room?

4. Jun took some apples from a bag. Show how many apples were in the bag originally.

   a)  –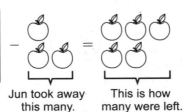

   Jun took away this many.   This is how many were left.

   b) 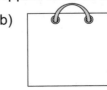 –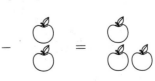

5. Show how many apples were in the bag originally. Then write an equation to represent the picture.

a)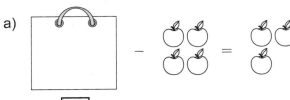

$\boxed{} - 4 = 3$

b)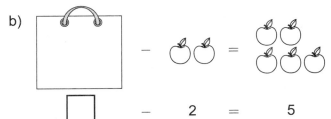

$\boxed{} - 2 = 5$

6. Find the number that makes the equation true and write it in the box.

a) $\boxed{6} + 3 = 9$

b) $\boxed{} + 4 = 9$

c) $\boxed{} + 5 = 9$

d) $8 - \boxed{} = 5$

e) $13 - \boxed{} = 11$

f) $19 - \boxed{} = 8$

g) $3 + 6 = 5 + \boxed{}$

h) $10 - 3 = \boxed{} + 4$

i) $1 + 5 = 7 - \boxed{}$

7. Draw the same number of apples in each box. Write the equation for the picture.

a) $\boxed{} + \boxed{} = 10$

_____

b)

_____

8. Draw a picture for the equation. Use your picture to solve the equation.

a) $3 \times \boxed{} = $

$3 \times \boxed{4} = 12$

b) $2 \times \boxed{} = $

$2 \times \boxed{} = 10$

c) $3 \times \boxed{} = $

$3 \times \boxed{} = 18$

d) $\boxed{} \times 6 = $

$\boxed{} \times 6 = 24$

9. How many apples should be in the box? Write the number.

a) $2 \times \boxed{3} = $ (apples)

b) $2 \times \boxed{} = $ (apples)

c) $\boxed{} \times 3 = $ (apples)

d) $\boxed{} \times 4 = $ (apples)

e) $3 \times$ (apples) $= \boxed{}$

f) $3 \times$ (apples) $= \boxed{}$

g) $8 \times$ (apples) $= \boxed{}$

h) $7 \times$ (apples) $= \boxed{}$

BONUS ▶ There are 13 apples in the bag. What number goes in the box?

$4 \times \left(\text{bag} + \text{apples} \right) = \boxed{}$

> Use circles instead of apples to make your drawing simpler.

10. Draw a picture of each equation. Then solve the equation using your picture.

a) $3 \times 4 = \boxed{}$

b) $3 \times \boxed{} = 18$

11. Solve the equation by guessing and checking.

a) $6 \times \boxed{} = 30$

b) $\boxed{} \times 2 = 18$

c) $2 \times \boxed{} = 24$

d) $\boxed{} \times 7 = 42$

e) $24 \div \boxed{} = 6$

f) $\boxed{} \div 5 = 6$

g) $5 \times 4 = \boxed{} \times 10$

h) $12 \times 3 = 9 \times \boxed{}$

12. Solve the equation by writing the unknown by itself.

a) $3 \times \boxed{} = 18$

b) $\boxed{} \times 7 = 28$

c) $\boxed{} \div 4 = 5$

d) $12 \div \boxed{} = 6$

e) $\boxed{} \times 8 = 32$

f) $\boxed{} \div 5 = 7$

g) $24 \div \boxed{} = 4$

h) $30 \div \boxed{} = 2$

PA5-10 Translating Words into Expressions

1. Match the description with the correct numerical expression.

   a) 2 more than 6 4×6

   6 divided by 3 $6 - 2$

   2 less than 6 $6 + 2$

   the product of 6 and 4 $6 - 3$

   6 decreased by 3 $6 \div 3$

   b) 2 divided into 11 3×11

   11 reduced by 4 $11 \div 2$

   11 times 3 $11 + 3$

   twice as many as 11 $11 - 4$

   11 increased by 3 2×11

2. Write an expression for each description.

   a) 4 more than 3 ___$3 + 4$___

   b) 15 decreased by 8 _____

   c) 24 divided by 8 _____

   d) 2 less than 9 ___$9 - 2$___

   e) 67 increased by 29 _____

   f) 35 added to 4 _____

   g) twice as many as 5 _____

   h) 15 divided by 5 _____

   i) the product of 7 and 4 _____

   j) 5 times 8 _____

3. Turn the written instructions into mathematical expressions.

   a) Add 8 and 3. ___$8 + 3$___

   b) Divide 6 by 2. _____

   c) Add 34 and 9. _____

   d) Subtract 5 from 7. _____

   e) Multiply 42 and 2. _____

   f) Decrease 3 by 2. _____

   g) Add 8 and 4. Then divide by 3. _____

   h) Divide 8 by 4. Then add 5. _____

   i) Divide 4 by 2. Then add 10. Then subtract 4. _____

   j) Multiply 6 and 5. Then subtract 20. Then divide by 2. _____

4. Write the mathematical expressions in words.

   a) $(6 + 2) \times 3$ ___Add 6 and 2. Then multiply by 3.___

   b) $(6 + 1) \times 2$ _____

   c) $12 - 5 \times 2$ _____

   d) $(3 - 2) \times 4$ _____

   BONUS ▶

   $4 \times (3 - 1 + 5)$ _____

5. How far will a motorcycle travel at the speed and in the time given? Write the numerical expression.

a) Speed: 60 km per hour
   Time: 2 hours

   Distance: ___60 × 2___ km

b) Speed: 80 km per hour
   Time: 4 hours

   Distance: _____ km

c) Speed: 70 km per hour
   Time: 5 hours

   Distance: _____ km

6. a) Look at the sign below, then write a numerical expression for the cost of renting a bike for …

   i) 1 hour: ___5 × 1___

   ii) 2 hours: _____

   iii) 4 hours: _____

   b) Complete the description of the expression.

   i) 5 × 3 is the cost of renting a bike for _3_ hours.

   ii) 5 × 2 is the cost of renting a bike for ____ hours.

   iii) 5 × 5 is the cost of renting a bike for ____ hours.

7. a) A different rental company charges $3 for each hour. Write the numerical expression for the cost of renting a bike for …

   i) 1 hour: ___3 × 1___

   ii) 2 hours: _____

   iii) 4 hours: _____

   b) Complete the description of the expression.

   i) 3 × 3 is the cost of renting a bike for _3_ hours.

   ii) 3 × 2 is the cost of renting a bike for ____ hours.

   iii) 3 × 5 is the cost of renting a bike for ____ hours.

8. A field trip for a Grade 5 class costs $11 per student plus $2 for a snack.

   a) Write an expression to represent the cost for 1 student and 1 snack. _____

   b) Write an expression to represent the cost for 3 students and 3 snacks. _____

   BONUS ▶ Write a word problem that could be represented by 19 × (11 + 2).

9. A day pass can be used by 2 adults and 2 children for unlimited one-day bus travel on weekends. Write an expression to represent the number of day passes that are needed for 10 adults and 10 children. Hint: The number of adults and the number of children are the same.

   BONUS ▶ 20 students from each class go to the museum. There are 5 classes, along with 13 teachers and 16 parents.

   a) Write an expression to represent the number of people who go to the museum.

   b) How many buses will be needed if 30 people ride in each bus?

PA5-11 Variables

1. Look at the sign at the right, then write a numerical expression for the cost of renting skates for …

a) 2 hours: __3 × 2__

b) 5 hours: _____

c) 6 hours: _____

d) 8 hours: _____

A **variable** is a letter or symbol (such as x, n, or H) that represents a number.

To make an **algebraic expression**, replace some numbers in a numerical expression with variables.

Examples of algebraic expressions: $x + 1$ $3 + 4 \times T$ $2 + t - 3 \times h$

---

2. Write an expression for the distance a car would travel at the given speed and time.

a) Speed: 60 km per hour

   Time: 2 hours

   Distance: _____ km

b) Speed: 80 km per hour

   Time: 3 hours

   Distance: _____ km

c) Speed: 70 km per hour

   Time: h hours

   Distance: _____ km

In the product of a number and a variable, the multiplication sign is usually dropped.

Examples: $3 \times T$ can be written $3T$ and $5 \times z$ can be written $5z$.

---

3. Look at the sign at the right, then write an algebraic expression for the cost of renting skis for …

a) h hours: __5 × h__ or __5h__

b) t hours: _____ or _____

c) x hours: _____ or _____

d) n hours: _____ or _____

4. Write an equation that tells you the relationship between the numbers in Column A and Column B. Hint: First find the number that you need to add or multiply.

a)

A	B
1	4
2	5
3	6

__A + 3 = B__

b)

A	B
1	2
2	4
3	6

__2 × A = B__
__or 2A = B__

c)

A	B
1	3
2	4
3	5

_____

d)

A	B
1	3
2	6
3	9

_____
_____

e)

A	B
1	5
2	10
3	15

_____
_____

When replacing a variable with a number, we use brackets.

Example: Replacing n with 7 in the expression $3n$ gives $3(7)$, which is another way to write 3×7.

5. Write the number 2 in the brackets and evaluate.

a) $5 (2) = \underline{5 \times 2} = \underline{10}$

b) $3 (\quad) = \underline{\hspace{1cm}} = \underline{\hspace{0.7cm}}$

c) $4 (\quad) = \underline{\hspace{1cm}} = \underline{\hspace{0.7cm}}$

d) $2 (\quad) + 5$

$= \underline{2 \times 2 + 5} = \underline{4 + 5}$

$= \underline{9}$

e) $4 (\quad) - 2$

$= \underline{\hspace{1.5cm}} = \underline{\hspace{0.7cm}}$

$= \underline{\hspace{0.7cm}}$

f) $6 (\quad) + 3$

$= \underline{\hspace{1.5cm}} = \underline{\hspace{0.7cm}}$

$= \underline{\hspace{0.7cm}}$

6. Replace n with 2 in each expression and evaluate.

a) $4n + 3$

$4(2) + 3$

$= 8 + 3 = 11$

b) $5n + 1$

c) $3n - 2$

d) $2n + 3$

e) $4n - 3$

f) $2n - 4$

7. Replace the variable with the given number and evaluate.

a) $5h + 2, \quad h = 3$

$5(3) + 2$

$= 15 + 2 = 17$

b) $2n + 3, \quad n = 6$

c) $5t - 2, \quad t = 4$

d) $3m + 9, \quad m = 8$

e) $9 - z, \quad z = 4$

f) $3n + 2, \quad n = 5$

8. Evaluate each expression.

a) $2n + 3, \quad n = 5$

$2(5) + 3$

$= 10 + 3 = 13$

b) $2t + 3, \quad t = 5$

c) $2w + 3, \quad w = 5$

9. What do you notice about your answers to Question 8? \underline{\hspace{5cm}}

Why is that so? \underline{\hspace{7cm}}

\underline{\hspace{10cm}}

PA5-12 Totals, Differences, and Equations

1. Fill in the table. Write x for the number you are not given.

		Blue Balloons	Red Balloons	Total Balloons	Another Way to Write the Total
a)	9 blue balloons 17 balloons in total	9	x	17	9 + x
b)	15 blue balloons 13 red balloons				
c)	31 balloons in total 18 blue balloons				
d)	17 red balloons 23 balloons altogether				
e)	34 red balloons 21 blue balloons				

When you can write the same number two ways, you can write an equation.

Example: 9 blue balloons, x red balloons, 17 balloons in total

Write the total two ways to get an equation: 9 + x = 17

2. Circle the total in the story. Then write an equation.

a) 15 blue balloons
    (28 balloons altogether)
    x red balloons

   $15 + x = 28$

b) 12 blue balloons
    14 red balloons
    x balloons altogether

   _____

c) 27 balloons altogether
    19 red balloons
    x blue balloons

   _____

d) There are 13 red apples.
    There are x green apples.
    There are 27 apples in total.

   _____

e) There are x red apples.
    There are 14 green apples.
    There are 39 apples in total.

   _____

f) There are 55 red apples.
    There are 16 green apples.
    There are x apples in total.

   _____

3. Circle the total in the story. Then write an equation and solve it.

a) There are 9 cats.
    There are 12 dogs.
    There are x pets altogether.

   _____

   _____

b) There are 19 stickers.
    x of them are black.
    11 of them are not black.

   _____

   _____

c) Kim has 9 friends.
    x of them are in Grade 6.
    6 friends are in Grade 5.

   _____

   _____

larger part − smaller part = difference

  9   − x =   4

9 is 4 more than x. x is 4 fewer than 9. So $x = 9 − 4$ and now the variable x is by itself.

4. Fill in the table. Write x for the number you are not given. Circle the larger part and then write the difference another way.

		Parts		Difference	Another Way to Write the Difference
		Apples	Oranges		
a)	13 apples, 5 more oranges than apples	13	(x)	5	$x − 13$
b)	9 more oranges than apples, 12 apples				
c)	6 apples, 7 oranges				
d)	19 oranges, 8 fewer apples than oranges				
e)	27 oranges, 13 fewer oranges than apples				

5. Circle the part that is larger. Write the difference two ways to make an equation.

a) (8 apples)
   3 fewer oranges than apples
   x oranges

   $\underline{8 − x = 3}$

b) 5 apples
   13 oranges
   x more oranges than apples

   _____

c) 12 more apples than oranges
   5 oranges
   x apples

   _____

6. Circle the part that is larger. Write the difference two ways to make an equation. Then solve the equation.

a) There are (7 games.)
   There are x books.
   There are 5 more games than books.

b) There are x games.
   There are 12 books.
   There are 6 fewer games than books.

c) There are 12 games.
   There are 29 books.
   There are x fewer games than books.

d) There are 17 pens.
   There are x pencils.
   There are 8 more pens than pencils.

e) Tom has 19 stickers.
   Avril has x stickers.
   Tom has 13 fewer stickers than Avril.

f) Eric's class has x students.
   Amy's class has 34 students.
   Eric's class has 6 fewer students than Amy's class.

7. Fill in the table. Write x for the number you are not given.

	Problem	Parts	How Many?	Equation and Solution
a)	Alex has 22 jazz songs in his collection. He has 8 more jazz songs than pop songs. How many pop songs does he have?	jazz songs	(22)	$22 - x = 8$ $22 - 8 = x$ $14 = x$
		pop songs	x	
b)	Dory has 21 red balloons. She has 9 green balloons. How many more red balloons than green balloons does she have?			
c)	There are 7 apples in the fridge. There are 4 more oranges than apples in the fridge. How many oranges are there?			
d)	Female European wolves weigh 4 kg less than male wolves. Males weigh 38 kg. How much do females weigh?			

8. Write the difference two ways to write an equation. Then solve the equation.

a) Simon exercised for 25 minutes on Saturday. On Sunday he exercised for 17 minutes more than on Saturday. For how long did he exercise on Sunday?

$$\underline{\qquad x - 25 = 17 \qquad}$$
$$\underline{\qquad x = 17 + 25 \qquad}$$
$$\underline{\qquad\qquad = 42 \qquad}$$

b) There are 32 teachers in the school. There are 18 fewer volunteers than teachers. How many volunteers are there?

$$\underline{\qquad\qquad\qquad\qquad}$$
$$\underline{\qquad\qquad\qquad\qquad}$$
$$\underline{\qquad\qquad\qquad\qquad}$$

c) North American wolves weigh 36 kg. Indian–Arabian wolves weigh 11 kg less. How much do Indian–Arabian wolves weigh?

d) Jasmin biked 13 km on Saturday. She biked 5 km more on Sunday than on Saturday. How many kilometres did she bike on Sunday?

e) Raj counted 68 cars in a parking lot on Monday and 39 cars on Tuesday. How many fewer cars were parked there on Tuesday?

BONUS ▸ Grace's art exhibition had 658 visitors on the first night. The next night, there were 18 more visitors than on the first night. How many visitors came on the second night?

PA5-13 Problems and Equations—Addition and Subtraction

1. Fill in the table. Write *x* for the number you need to find. Cross out the cell you do not use.

	Problem	Parts	How Many?	Difference / Total	Equation and Solution
a)	Ethan has 2 dogs and 5 fish. How many pets does he have?	*dogs*	2	Difference: ~~✗~~	2 + 5 = x
		fish	5	Total: _x_	x = 7
b)	Sharon hiked 9 km on Saturday. She hiked 12 km on Sunday. How far did Sharon hike in two days?			Difference: _____	
				Total: _____	
c)	Luc saved $36 in January. He saved $17 less in February than in January. How much money did he save in February?			Difference: _____	
				Total: _____	
d)	The Leviathan roller coaster is 93 m tall. It is 25 m taller than the Yukon Striker roller coaster. How tall is the Yukon Striker?			Difference: _____	
				Total: _____	
e)	A supermarket sold 164 bags of white and yellow potatoes. If 76 of the bags were filled with white potatoes, how many bags of yellow potatoes were sold?			Difference: _____	
				Total: _____	

2. Write the parts and how many of each part. Then write and solve an equation.

   a) Cam has 12 blue marbles. He has 9 more red marbles than blue marbles. How many red marbles does he have?

   b) Cam also has 7 fewer green marbles than red marbles. How many green marbles does he have?

   c) How many red, blue, and green marbles does Cam have altogether? _____

Write an equation to solve the problems on this page.

3. There are 32 children in a class. 13 of them wear eyeglasses.

   a) How many students don't wear eyeglasses?

   b) How many more students are there who don't wear eyeglasses than students who wear eyeglasses?

4. Rani bought 8 hockey cards and 10 baseball cards. She gave away 3 cards.

   a) How many cards did she buy altogether?

   b) How many cards does she have left?

5. Neka is three years older than Megan. Megan is 9 years old. How old is Neka?

6. Anton bought a science-fiction novel for $11 and a graphic novel for $7.

   a) How much more expensive is the science-fiction novel than the graphic novel?

   b) How much did the books cost in total?

7. Nina watched TV for 60 minutes. She spent 20 minutes less on her homework than on watching TV. How much time did she spend on homework?

8. A recreation pass costs $23. It is $8 more than a movie pass. How much does the movie pass cost?

9. The Willis Tower in Chicago, USA, is 442 m tall. The CN Tower in Toronto is 553 m tall. How much taller is the CN Tower than the Willis Tower?

Willis Tower   CN Tower

PA5-14 Models and "Times as Many"

1. Draw a diagram to model the story.

   a) Sally has 7 stickers. Jake has 3 times as many stickers as Sally does.

      Sally's stickers _____ | 7 |

      Jake's stickers _____ | 7 | 7 | 7 |

   b) There are 5 blue marbles. There are 4 times as many red marbles.

      _____

      _____

   c) There are 12 red apples. There are 4 times as many green apples as red apples.

      _____

      _____

   d) Yu has 4 stickers. Nora has 5 times as many stickers.

      _____

      _____

2. Solve the problem by drawing a model.

   a) Jin has 5 stickers. Rob has 3 times as many stickers as Jin. How many stickers do they have together?

      Jin's stickers: 5 _____ | 5 |

      Rob's stickers: 15 _____ | 5 | 5 | 5 |

      5 + 15 = 20, so Jin and Rob have _____

      20 stickers altogether. _____

   b) Randi studies rats and hamsters. She has 7 rats and twice as many hamsters. How many animals does she have altogether?

      _____

      _____

      _____

      _____

   c) There are 12 chocolate chip cookies in a box. There are 6 times as many oatmeal cookies in the box. How many cookies are there altogether?

   d) There are 17 math books in a school library. There are 4 times as many science books in the library. How many math books and science books are in the library altogether?

3. Draw a model for the story. Then write the given number beside the correct bar.

   a) There are 24 mangoes. There are 4 times as many mangoes as avocados.

      Mangoes: 24 _____ | | | | |

      Avocados: _____ | |

   b) There are 30 seniors in the audience. There are 6 times as many seniors as children.

      _____

      _____

   c) Matt spent $24 on shoes and twice as much on pants.

      _____

      _____

   d) Abella studied math for 30 minutes and science for 3 times as many minutes.

      _____

      _____

4. All the blocks are the same size. What is the size of each block?

a)

7	7	7	7

7	21

b)

	32

c)

total: 36

d)

total: 48

5. Draw the model. Find the length of one block in the model. Then solve the problem.

a) Jay has 3 times as many cards as Sam. Jay has 12 more cards than Sam. How many cards does each person have?

Jay's cards

6	6	6

Sam's cards

6	12

Jay has __18__ cards

and Sam has __6__ cards.

b) Vicky is 4 times as old as Ella. Vicky is 15 years older than Ella. How old are Vicky and Ella?

_____

_____

Vicky is ____ years old

and Ella is ____ years old.

BONUS ▶
A pancake recipe calls for 2 tablespoons of butter and 3 times as many tablespoons of sugar per batch. Anna wants to make 24 batches. How many tablespoons of sugar and butter does she need?

c) There are 6 times as many party balloons as streamers to decorate a house. There are 42 decorations altogether. How many balloons and how many streamers are there?

There are ____ party balloons

and ____ streamers.

Anna needs ____ tablespoons of butter and

____ tablespoons of sugar.

6. A pair of shoes costs twice as much as a wallet. Glen paid $51 for a pair of shoes and a wallet. How much does each item cost?

_____

_____

BONUS ▶ How much would Glen pay for two pairs of shoes and three wallets?

PA5-15 Problems and Equations—Multiplication and Division

When the larger part is 3 times the size of the smaller part, we say the **scale factor** is 3.

Smaller Part

Larger Part

You can find one part from another part using the scale factor.

Larger Part = Smaller Part × Scale Factor

Smaller Part = Larger Part ÷ Scale Factor

1. Circle the larger part and underline the smaller part in the problem. Then fill in the blanks for the equation where the unknown is by itself and cross out the other equation.

   a) There are 21 cats and *m* dogs. There are three times as many (dogs) as cats.

      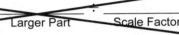

$\underline{\quad m \quad}$	=	$\underline{\quad 21 \quad}$	×	$\underline{\quad 3 \quad}$	or	~~$\underline{\qquad}$~~	~~=~~	~~$\underline{\qquad}$~~	÷	~~$\underline{\qquad}$~~
Larger Part		Smaller Part		Scale Factor		~~Smaller Part~~		~~Larger Part~~		~~Scale Factor~~

   b) There are *m* cats and 6 dogs. There are 3 times as many dogs as cats.

$\underline{\qquad}$	=	$\underline{\qquad}$	×	$\underline{\qquad}$	or	$\underline{\qquad}$	=	$\underline{\qquad}$	÷	$\underline{\qquad}$
Larger Part		Smaller Part		Scale Factor		Smaller Part		Larger Part		Scale Factor

   c) There are 12 cars in a parking lot. There are twice as many vans as cars in the parking lot.

$\underline{\qquad}$	=	$\underline{\qquad}$	×	$\underline{\qquad}$	or	$\underline{\qquad}$	=	$\underline{\qquad}$	÷	$\underline{\qquad}$
Larger Part		Smaller Part		Scale Factor		Smaller Part		Larger Part		Scale Factor

2. Fill in the table. Write *n* for the number you are not given.
   Hint: Circle the larger part and underline the smaller part.

	Problem	Parts	How Many?	Equation
a)	There are 20 green apples in a box. There are 4 times as many (green apples) as red apples.	green apples	20	$20 \div 4 = n$
		red apples	n	
b)	There are 16 mangoes. There are twice as many mangoes as kiwis.			
c)	There are 6 cats in a shelter. There are three times as many dogs as cats in the shelter.			

3. Complete the table.

	Total Number of Things	Number of Sets	Number in Each Set	Multiplication or Division Equation
a)	p	5	2	$5 \times 2 = p$
b)	12	4	p	$12 \div 4 = p$
c)	14	p	7	
d)	p	2	11	

4. Fill in the table. Write *x* to show what you don't know. Then write a multiplication or division equation in the last column and solve the equation.

		Total Number of Things	Number of Sets	Number in Each Set	Multiplication or Division Equation
a)	24 people 4 vans	24	4	*x*	$24 \div 4 = x$ ___6___ people in each van
b)	8 balloons in each bag 5 bags				_____ _____ balloons
c)	35 students 7 teams				_____ _____ students on each team
d)	9 books on each shelf 6 shelves				_____ _____ books
e)	6 juice boxes in each pack 48 juice boxes				_____ _____ packs of juice

5. A store sold 6 rats and twice as many hamsters.

  a) How many hamsters did the store sell?

  b) How many rats and hamsters were sold altogether?

  c) How many more hamsters than rats were sold?

6. Emma is 5 times as old as Eddy. Emma is 35.

  a) How old is Eddy?

  b) How much older than Eddy is Emma?

7. A female angler fish is 5 times as large as a male angler fish.
The female can be 100 cm long.

  a) How long is the male angler fish?

  b) How much longer than the male is the female angler fish?

PA5-16 More Problems and Equations

1. a) There are 12 blue beads. There are 3 times as many blue beads as red beads.
        There are 7 fewer yellow beads than blue beads.

        How many red beads are there? _____   How many yellow beads are there? _____

    b) Ronin is 3 times as old as Liz. Karen is four years older than Liz. Liz is 6 years old.

        How old is Ronin? _____   How old is Karen? _____

2. Zara is two years older than Tristan. Tristan is 10 years old. Tristan is 7 years older
    than Carl. How old are Zara and Carl?

    Zara is _____ years old and Carl is _____ years old.

3. Ansel bought six books about mammals and two books about reptiles.
    Each book cost $12.

    a) How many books did Ansel buy altogether? _____

    b) How much did the books cost? _____

4. Aputik bought 7 books and 10 magazines. (See the prices in the picture.)

    a) How much did Aputik spend on books? _____

    b) How much did Aputik spend on magazines? _____

    c) How much did Aputik spend altogether? _____

5. What question do you need to ask and answer before you can solve the problem?

    a) Mary has twice as many hockey cards as Ren does. Mary has 10 more hockey
        cards than David. David has 16 hockey cards. How many cards does Ren have?

        How many cards does Mary have? _____

    b) Ben is twice as old as Lela. Lela is three years older than John.
        John is five years old. How old is Ben?

        _____

    c) Ryder had $53. He spent $15 on a hat, $8 on a scarf, and $12 on a pair of mitts.
        How much money does Ryder have left?

        _____

6. Tina earns $15 per hour. She worked 3 hours on Friday, 2 hours on Saturday,
    and 2 hours on Sunday. How much money did Tina earn in these three days?

7. Ava used 3 times as many blue beads as red beads for a bracelet.
She used 12 more blue beads than yellow beads. She used 3 yellow beads.

   a) How many beads of each colour did Ava use?

   b) How many beads did she use in total?

8. Snow geese can fly 160 km in 2 hours. They can fly for a very long time.

   a) Some snow geese flew for 18 hours, rested, and then flew for
      another 20 hours. How long did the geese travel? How far did
      the geese travel?

   b) Snow geese need to fly about 3200 km from British Columbia, Canada
      to Texas, USA. How much flying time do the geese need?

9. A narwhal is an arctic whale. The adult male has one very long tooth.
An adult narwhal is about 5 m long from nose to tail, and its tooth
is 3 m long. Use the diagram to tell how long a baby narwhal is.

adult male narwhal

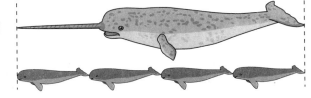

baby narwhal

10. An eraser is 5 cm long. A pencil is 15 cm long.
Write your answer as a full sentence.

   a) How many times as long as the eraser is the pencil?

   b) How many centimetres longer is the pencil than the eraser?

11. An elephant weighs 4000 kg and is 4 m tall.
Is this elephant 1000 times as heavy as it is tall? Explain.

12. There are 5 people at a pizza party. They ordered 2 pizzas.
Each pizza has 8 slices. Each person gets the same number
of slices. How many slices can each person have?

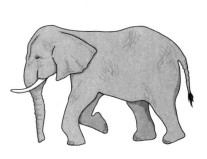

13. There are 52 avocados in a crate. Thirteen are spoiled. Zack packs
the rest into bags of 5 avocados. How many full bags can he make?

14. There are 24 students in one class and 23 students in another class
going on a field trip. Each car can hold 4 students. How many cars are
needed to transport all the students?

NS5-34 Naming Fractions—Area

> The whole pie is cut into 4 equal parts.
>
> 3 parts out of 4 are shaded.
>
> $\frac{3}{4}$ of the whole pie is shaded.
>
> 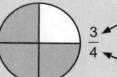 $\frac{3}{4}$
>
> The **numerator** (3) tells you how many parts are shaded.
>
> The **denominator** (4) tells you how many equal parts are in a whole.

1. Name the fraction.

a) $\frac{3}{8}$

b)

c)

d)

e)

f)

g)

h)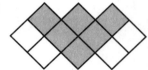

2. Shade the given fraction.

a) $\frac{4}{6}$

b) $\frac{2}{5}$

c) $\frac{7}{20}$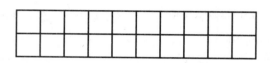

3. Use one of the following words to describe the parts in the model.

halves   thirds   fourths   fifths   sixths   sevenths   eighths   ninths

a)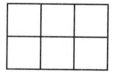

_____sixths_____

b)

_____

c)

_____

d)

_____

e)

_____

f)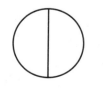

_____

4. Sketch a circle cut into …

a) thirds.

b) quarters (or fourths).

c) eighths.

5. Use a centimetre ruler to divide the line into equal parts. The first one is started for you.

a) 5 equal parts

b) 8 equal parts

_____

c) 6 equal parts

_____

6. Using a ruler, join the marks to divide the box into equal parts.

a) 4 equal parts

b) 5 equal parts

7. Mark the box in centimetres. Then divide the box into equal parts.

a) 3 equal parts

b) 6 equal parts

8. Using a ruler, find what fraction of the box is shaded.

a)

is shaded.

b)

is shaded.

9. Using a ruler, complete the figure to make a whole.

a) $\frac{1}{2}$

b) $\frac{2}{3}$

10. You have $\frac{3}{8}$ of a whole pie.

a) What does the bottom (denominator) of the fraction tell you?

_____

b) What does the top (numerator) of the fraction tell you?

_____

11. Explain why the picture does (or does not) show $\frac{1}{4}$.

a)   b)   c)   BONUS ▶

NS5-35 Naming Fractions—Sets

Fractions can name or describe parts of a set. Example:

$\frac{3}{5}$ of the shapes are triangles, $\frac{1}{5}$ are squares, $\frac{1}{5}$ are circles.

1. Complete the sentence.

   a) $\frac{4}{7}$ of the shapes are _____.

   b) $\frac{2}{7}$ of the shapes are _____.

   c) $\frac{1}{7}$ of the shapes are _____.

   d) $\frac{3}{7}$ of the shapes are _____.

2. Complete the sentences.

   a)

     ☐ of the shapes are squares.

     ☐ of the shapes are shaded.

   b)

     ☐ of the shapes are triangles.

     ☐ of the shapes are unshaded.

3. Describe the picture in two different ways using the fraction $\frac{3}{5}$.

_____

_____

4. A football team wins 6 games and loses 3 games.

   a) How many games did the team play? _____

   b) What fraction of the games did the team win? ☐

   c) What fraction of the games did the team lose? ☐

   d) Did the team win more than half its games? _____

5. Answer the question using the information in the table.

a) What fraction of the students in each class have siblings?

Class A ☐   Class B ☐

	Has Siblings	Has No Siblings
Class A	2	3
Class B	1	2

b) What fraction of all the students have siblings? ☐

6. What fraction of the letters in the word "Manitoba" are …

a) vowels? ☐

b) consonants? ☐

7. Express 6 days as a fraction of one week. ☐

8.

a) ☐ of the shapes are circles.

b) ☐ of the shapes are triangles.

c) ☐ of the shapes are striped.

d) ☐ of the shapes are white.

9. Write two more fraction statements for the figures in Question 8.

☐ of the shapes are _____.

☐ of the shapes are _____.

10. Draw the shaded and unshaded shapes and then answer the question.

a) There are 7 circles and squares.

$\frac{4}{7}$ of the shapes are squares.

$\frac{5}{7}$ of the shapes are shaded.

3 circles are shaded.

How many squares are shaded?

b) There are 8 triangles and squares.

$\frac{3}{8}$ of the shapes are shaded.

$\frac{4}{8}$ of the shapes are triangles.

1 triangle is shaded.

How many squares are not shaded?

NS5-36 Comparing Fractions (Introduction)

1. Which strip has more shading? Circle its fraction.

a)  $\dfrac{2}{3}$

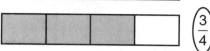 $\left(\dfrac{3}{4}\right)$

b) 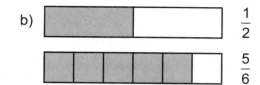 $\dfrac{1}{2}$

$\dfrac{5}{6}$

c) 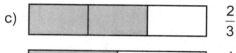 $\dfrac{2}{3}$

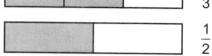 $\dfrac{1}{2}$

d) 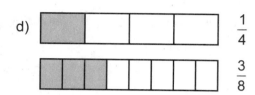 $\dfrac{1}{4}$

$\dfrac{3}{8}$

e) 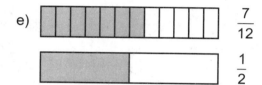 $\dfrac{7}{12}$

$\dfrac{1}{2}$

f) 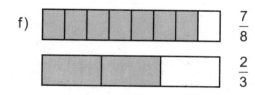 $\dfrac{7}{8}$

$\dfrac{2}{3}$

The strip with more shading represents the greater fraction. $\dfrac{1}{2}$ has more shading than $\dfrac{1}{3}$. So $\dfrac{1}{2}$ is **greater than** $\dfrac{1}{3}$.

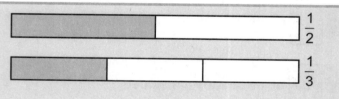 $\dfrac{1}{2}$

$\dfrac{1}{3}$

2. Shade the amounts given by the fractions. Circle the greater fraction.

a)  $\dfrac{2}{3}$

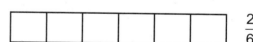 $\dfrac{2}{6}$

b) $\dfrac{1}{2}$

 $\dfrac{1}{8}$

c) 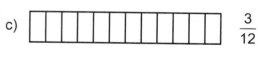 $\dfrac{3}{12}$

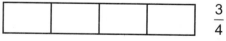 $\dfrac{3}{4}$

d) $\dfrac{2}{4}$

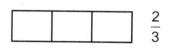 $\dfrac{2}{3}$

e) 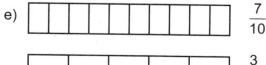 $\dfrac{7}{10}$

$\dfrac{3}{5}$

f) $\dfrac{3}{4}$

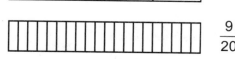 $\dfrac{9}{20}$

3. Shade the amounts given by the fractions. Circle the greater fraction. Write > or < between the fractions.

a) 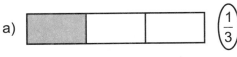 $\left(\dfrac{1}{3}\right)$

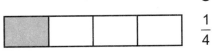 $\dfrac{1}{4}$

 $\dfrac{1}{3} \;\boxed{>}\; \dfrac{1}{4}$

b) 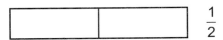 $\dfrac{3}{8}$

$\dfrac{1}{2}$

$\dfrac{3}{8} \;\boxed{}\; \dfrac{1}{2}$

c) 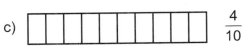 $\dfrac{4}{10}$

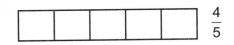 $\dfrac{4}{5}$

$\dfrac{4}{10} \;\boxed{}\; \dfrac{4}{5}$

d) 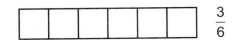 $\dfrac{2}{3}$

$\dfrac{3}{6}$

$\dfrac{2}{3} \;\boxed{}\; \dfrac{3}{6}$

e) 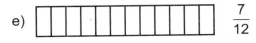 $\dfrac{7}{12}$

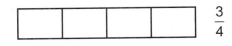 $\dfrac{3}{4}$

$\dfrac{7}{12} \;\boxed{}\; \dfrac{3}{4}$

f) 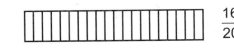 $\dfrac{3}{4}$

$\dfrac{16}{20}$

$\dfrac{3}{4} \;\boxed{}\; \dfrac{16}{20}$

BONUS ▶ Shade the strips to show that Jin ate $\dfrac{2}{3}$ of his fruit strip, Simon ate $\dfrac{9}{12}$ of his fruit strip, and Alexa ate $\dfrac{14}{24}$ of her fruit strip. Who ate the largest amount of the fruit strip? Order the fractions from greatest to least in the blanks below.

Jin:

Simon:

Alexa:

$\boxed{} \;>\; \boxed{} \;>\; \boxed{}$

Number Sense 5-36

NS5-37 Fractions and Number Lines

1. Write a scale below the number line. Use it to find what fraction of the number line from 0 to 1 is shaded.

a)

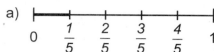

$\boxed{\dfrac{1}{5}}$ is shaded.

So $\boxed{}$ is shaded.

b)

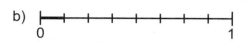

$\boxed{}$ is shaded.

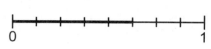

So $\boxed{}$ is shaded.

You can use number lines to compare and order fractions.

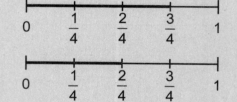

$\dfrac{3}{4}$ is greater than $\dfrac{2}{4}$ because it is farther to the right: $\dfrac{3}{4} > \dfrac{2}{4}$.

---

2. Find what fraction of each number line from 0 to 1 is shaded. Then compare the fractions in the blanks below.

a)

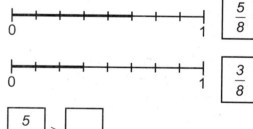

$\boxed{\dfrac{5}{8}}$

$\boxed{\dfrac{3}{8}}$

$\boxed{\dfrac{5}{8}} > \boxed{}$

b)

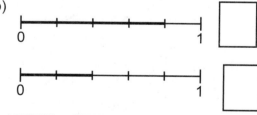

$\boxed{}$

$\boxed{}$

$\boxed{} > \boxed{}$

3. Use the number line to order the fractions from least to greatest.
    Draw an ✗ to mark the position of each fraction.

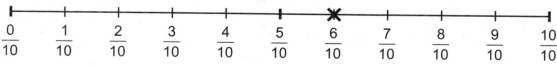

$\dfrac{6}{10} \quad \dfrac{3}{10} \quad \dfrac{8}{10} \quad \dfrac{4}{10} \quad \dfrac{1}{10} \quad \dfrac{9}{10} \quad \dfrac{7}{10}$

$\boxed{} < \boxed{} < \boxed{} < \boxed{} < \boxed{} < \boxed{} < \boxed{}$

4. $\frac{3}{4}$ of the top strip is shaded and $\frac{2}{3}$ of the bottom strip is shaded. Both lengths are marked on the same number line.

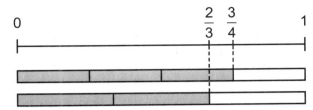

Which fraction is bigger? ☐

5. Use the fractions marked on the number line to answer the question.

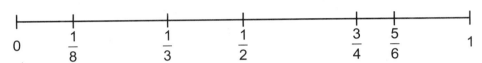

a) Write < (less than) or > (greater than).

i) $\frac{1}{8}$ ☐ $\frac{1}{2}$

ii) $\frac{3}{4}$ ☐ $\frac{1}{3}$

iii) $\frac{5}{6}$ ☐ $\frac{3}{4}$

b) Circle these fractions on the number line above. Then write them from greatest to least.

$\frac{1}{2}$, $\frac{5}{6}$, $\frac{1}{3}$ ☐ > ☐ > ☐

c) You can see from the number line that $\frac{1}{8}$ is less than $\frac{1}{3}$, which is less than $\frac{1}{2}$.

Explain why the fraction with the largest denominator is the smallest of the three fractions. Explain why the fraction with the smallest denominator is the largest of the three fractions.

Two fractions that mark the same place on a number line from 0 to 1 represent the same amount.

6. Use the number lines to find the missing number.

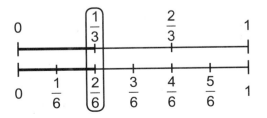
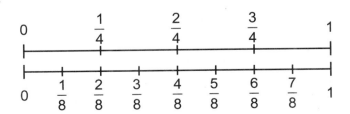

a) $\frac{1}{3} = \frac{2}{6}$

b) $\frac{2}{3} = \frac{}{6}$

c) $\frac{1}{4} = \frac{}{8}$

d) $\frac{3}{4} = \frac{}{8}$

1. a) Write the numerators of the shaded fractions.

$$\frac{}{4} \qquad\qquad \frac{}{4} \qquad\qquad \frac{}{4}$$

b) Look at the pictures and fractions in part a) from left to right. Write "increases," "decreases," or "stays the same."

i) The numerator _____.

ii) The denominator _____.

iii) The shaded fraction _____.

Comparing fractions when ...

the numerator changes and **the denominator stays the same**

$$\frac{1}{5}$$

fewer shaded parts → ← same number and size of parts

more shaded parts → ←

$$\frac{2}{5}$$

So $\frac{2}{5} > \frac{1}{5}$ because more parts are shaded.

---

2. Circle the greater fraction.

a) $\frac{3}{5}$ or $\frac{4}{5}$

b) $\frac{3}{4}$ or $\frac{1}{4}$

c) $\frac{4}{12}$ or $\frac{9}{12}$

d) $\frac{3}{3}$ or $\frac{1}{3}$

3. Write any number in the blank that makes the relationship correct.

a) $\frac{3}{7} > \frac{}{7}$

b) $\frac{}{29} < \frac{21}{29}$

c) $\frac{61}{385} > \frac{}{385}$

BONUS ▶ $\frac{}{1000} < \frac{2}{1000}$

4. Two fractions have the same denominator but different numerators. How can you tell which fraction is greater?

_____

_____

5. Order the fractions from least to greatest by considering the numerators and denominators.

a) $\dfrac{3}{5}$ $\dfrac{0}{5}$ $\dfrac{2}{5}$ $\dfrac{5}{5}$ $\dfrac{1}{5}$

b) $\dfrac{6}{10}$ $\dfrac{1}{10}$ $\dfrac{4}{10}$ $\dfrac{2}{10}$ $\dfrac{9}{10}$

☐ < ☐ < ☐ < ☐ < ☐   ☐ < ☐ < ☐ < ☐ < ☐

6. a) What fraction of a litre is in the container?

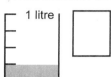 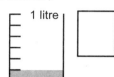 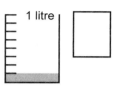

b) Which fraction in part a) is …

i) the smallest? ☐   ii) the biggest? ☐   iii) in the middle? ☐

c) Write "smaller" or "bigger." As the denominator gets bigger, each part gets _____.

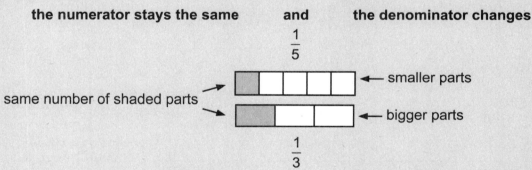

Comparing fractions when ...

the numerator stays the same and **the denominator changes**

$\dfrac{1}{5}$

same number of shaded parts → ← smaller parts

← bigger parts

$\dfrac{1}{3}$

So $\dfrac{1}{5} < \dfrac{1}{3}$ because the parts are smaller in the shape with more parts.

7. Circle the greater fraction.

a) $\dfrac{4}{5}$ or $\dfrac{4}{8}$ b) $\dfrac{3}{4}$ or $\dfrac{3}{5}$ c) $\dfrac{9}{15}$ or $\dfrac{9}{100}$ d) $\dfrac{3}{4}$ or $\dfrac{3}{3}$

8. Two fractions have the same numerator but different denominators.
How can you tell which fraction is greater?

_____

_____

9. a) Order the fractions from least to greatest by matching each fraction to the strip it represents and then shading it.

i) $\dfrac{1}{4}$ $\dfrac{1}{10}$ $\dfrac{1}{2}$ $\dfrac{1}{5}$ $\dfrac{1}{3}$

ii) $\dfrac{2}{2}$ $\dfrac{2}{4}$ $\dfrac{2}{10}$ $\dfrac{2}{3}$ $\dfrac{2}{5}$

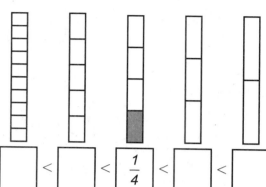
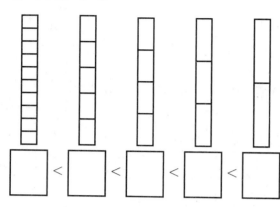

b) Order the fractions from least to greatest by considering the numerators and denominators.

i) $\dfrac{1}{4}$ $\dfrac{1}{10}$ $\dfrac{1}{2}$ $\dfrac{1}{5}$ $\dfrac{1}{3}$

ii) $\dfrac{2}{2}$ $\dfrac{2}{4}$ $\dfrac{2}{10}$ $\dfrac{2}{3}$ $\dfrac{2}{5}$

c) Are your answers for parts a) and b) the same? Explain.

_____

_____

10. Randi says that $\dfrac{1}{4}$ of a pie is less than $\dfrac{1}{6}$ of a pie. Is she correct? Explain.

_____

_____

11. Ray, Hanna, and Lynn each brought 1 pie to school. None of the pies are the same size. The teacher cut each pie into 9 equal pieces so that everyone in the class can have a piece. Ray says, "That's not fair at all!" and Lynn says, "That's perfectly fair!"

a) Why does Ray think it's unfair?

_____

_____

b) Why does Lynn think it's fair?

_____

_____

NS5-39 Equivalent Fractions

1. How many times as many parts are there?

a) has _____ times as many parts as .

b) has _____ times as many parts as .

c) has _____ times as many parts as .

d) has _____ times as many parts as .

2. Fill in the blanks.

a) A has _____ times as many parts as B.

   A has _____ times as many shaded parts as B.

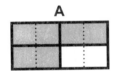

b) A has _____ times as many parts as B.

   A has _____ times as many shaded parts as B.

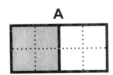 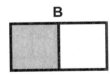

c) A has _____ times as many parts as B.

   A has _____ times as many shaded parts as B.

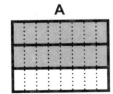 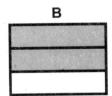

d) A has _____ times as many parts as B.

   A has _____ times as many shaded parts as B.

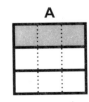

Equivalent fractions are fractions that have the same value or represent the same amount.

3. The picture shows two equivalent fractions. Use the picture to fill in the blanks.

a)  $\frac{3}{5}$ and $\frac{6}{10}$

6 is __2__ times as much as 3.

10 is _____ times as much as 5.

b)  $\frac{4}{5}$ and $\frac{12}{15}$

12 is _____ times as much as 4.

15 is _____ times as much as 5.

c)  $\frac{1}{4}$ and $\frac{2}{8}$

2 is _____ times as much as 1.

8 is _____ times as much as 4.

d) 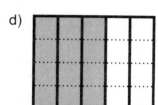 $\frac{3}{5}$ and $\frac{12}{20}$

12 is _____ times as much as 3.

20 is _____ times as much as 5.

4. Write an equivalent fraction for the picture. Then write how many times as much the new numerator and denominator are.

a) 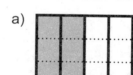 $\frac{2}{4} = \boxed{\frac{6}{12}}$

__3__ times as much

b) 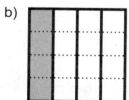 $\frac{1}{4} = \boxed{}$

_____ times as much

c) 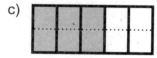 $\frac{3}{5} = \boxed{}$

_____ times as much

BONUS ▶

$\frac{7}{10} = \boxed{}$

_____ times as much

To get an equivalent fraction, multiply the numerator **and** denominator by the same number.

Example: Picture A   Picture B

$$\frac{3}{4} \xrightarrow[\times 2]{\times 2} \frac{6}{8}$$

Picture B has twice as many **parts** as Picture A.
Picture B has twice as many **shaded parts** as Picture A.

5. Draw lines to cut the whole pies into more equal pieces. Fill in the numerators of the equivalent fractions.

a)

4 pieces   6 pieces   8 pieces

$$\frac{1}{2} = \frac{}{4} = \frac{}{6} = \frac{}{8}$$

b)

6 pieces   9 pieces   12 pieces

$$\frac{1}{3} = \frac{}{6} = \frac{}{9} = \frac{}{12}$$

6. Draw lines to cut the whole pie into more pieces. Then fill in the missing numbers.

a)
   $\frac{2}{3} \xrightarrow[\times 2]{\times 2} \frac{}{6}$

b)
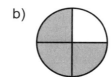 $\frac{3}{4} \xrightarrow[\times]{\times} \frac{}{8}$

c)
   $\frac{2}{3} \xrightarrow[\times]{\times} \frac{}{9}$

This number tells you how many pieces to cut each slice into.

7. Use multiplication to find the equivalent fraction.

a) $\dfrac{1 \times 2}{5 \times 2} = \dfrac{}{10}$

b) $\dfrac{1 \times}{2 \times} = \dfrac{}{10}$

c) $\dfrac{2}{5} = \dfrac{}{10}$

d) $\dfrac{3}{4} = \dfrac{}{8}$

e) $\dfrac{1}{4} = \dfrac{}{12}$

f) $\dfrac{4}{5} = \dfrac{}{15}$

g) $\dfrac{5}{6} = \dfrac{}{12}$

h) $\dfrac{8}{10} = \dfrac{}{100}$

i) $\dfrac{5}{9} = \dfrac{}{72}$

8. Write five fractions equivalent to $\dfrac{2}{5}$.

$$\frac{2}{5} = \boxed{} = \boxed{} = \boxed{} = \boxed{} = \boxed{}$$

Number Sense 5-39

NS5-40 Comparing Fractions Using Equivalent Fractions

1. Draw lines to cut the whole pies into more equal pieces. Then fill in the numerators of the equivalent fractions.

   a)

   $$\frac{2}{3} = \frac{}{6} = \frac{}{9} = \frac{}{12} = \frac{}{15}$$

   b)

   $$\frac{3}{5} = \frac{}{10} = \frac{}{15} = \frac{}{20} = \frac{}{25}$$

2. a) Write two fractions with the same denominator. Hint: Use your answers from Question 1.

   $\frac{2}{3} = \boxed{}$ and $\frac{3}{5} = \boxed{}$

   b) Which of the two fractions is greater, $\frac{2}{3}$ or $\frac{3}{5}$? $\boxed{}$

   How do you know? _____

   _____

3. Rewrite the fractions so that they have the same denominator. Then circle the larger fraction.

   a) $\frac{1}{3} = \frac{}{15}$ and $\frac{2}{5} = \frac{}{15}$ b) $\frac{3}{8} = \frac{}{24}$ and $\frac{1}{3} = \frac{}{24}$

4. a) Write an equivalent fraction with denominator 24.

   i) $\frac{2}{3} = \frac{}{24}$ ii) $\frac{5}{6} = \frac{}{24}$ iii) $\frac{3}{4} = \frac{}{24}$ iv) $\frac{1}{2} = \frac{}{24}$

   b) Write the fractions from part a) in order from least to greatest.

   $\boxed{} < \boxed{} < \boxed{} < \boxed{}$

5. Draw lines to cut the left-hand pie into the same number of equal pieces as the right-hand pie. Complete the equivalent fraction. Then circle the greater fraction.

a)

$$\frac{1}{2} = \frac{}{4} \qquad\qquad \frac{1}{4}$$

b)

$$\frac{2}{3} = \frac{}{6} \qquad\qquad \frac{5}{6}$$

6. Turn the fraction on the left into an equivalent fraction with the same denominator as the fraction on the right. Then write < (less than) or > (greater than) to show which fraction is greater.

a) $\dfrac{1 \times 3}{2 \times 3} = \dfrac{3}{6} \;\square\; \dfrac{4}{6}$

b) $\dfrac{3 \;\times}{4 \;\times} = \dfrac{}{8} \;\square\; \dfrac{5}{8}$

c) $\dfrac{1}{2} = \dfrac{}{} \;\square\; \dfrac{3}{4}$

d) $\dfrac{1}{3} = \dfrac{}{} \;\square\; \dfrac{2}{9}$

e) $\dfrac{3}{5} = \dfrac{}{} \;\square\; \dfrac{7}{10}$

BONUS ▶ $\dfrac{2}{5} = \dfrac{}{} \;\square\; \dfrac{17}{40}$

To compare $\dfrac{1}{3}$ and $\dfrac{2}{5}$ you can change them into fractions with the same denominator.

Multiply the numerator and denominator of each fraction by the denominator of the other fraction.

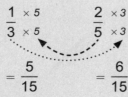

$$\dfrac{1 \times 5}{3 \times 5} \qquad \dfrac{2 \times 3}{5 \times 3}$$

$$= \dfrac{5}{15} \qquad = \dfrac{6}{15}$$

Now the fractions are easy to compare: $\dfrac{5}{15} < \dfrac{6}{15}$, so $\dfrac{1}{3} < \dfrac{2}{5}$.

---

7. Turn the fractions into fractions with the same denominator. Then compare the fractions. Show your answer using < or >.

a) $\dfrac{7 \times 3}{7 \times 4} \qquad \dfrac{5 \times 4}{7 \times 4}$

b) $\dfrac{\times 1}{\times 2} \qquad \dfrac{2 \times}{3 \times}$

c) $\dfrac{\times 1}{\times 2} \qquad \dfrac{3 \times}{4 \times}$

d) $\dfrac{\times 2}{\times 3} \qquad \dfrac{5 \times}{8 \times}$

$$= \dfrac{}{28} \quad = \dfrac{}{28} \qquad = \dfrac{}{} \quad = \dfrac{}{} \qquad = \dfrac{}{} \quad = \dfrac{}{} \qquad = \dfrac{}{} \quad = \dfrac{}{}$$

so $\dfrac{3}{4} \;\square\; \dfrac{5}{7}$ so $\dfrac{1}{2} \;\square\; \dfrac{2}{3}$ so $\dfrac{1}{2} \;\square\; \dfrac{3}{4}$ so $\dfrac{2}{3} \;\square\; \dfrac{5}{8}$

8. Draw a picture to justify your answer to Question 7.c).

NS5-41 Mixed Numbers and Improper Fractions (Introduction)

Matt and his friends ate the amount of pie shown.

They ate three and one quarter pies altogether (or $3\frac{1}{4}$ pies).

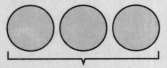

3 whole pies   *and $\frac{1}{4}$ of another pie*

$3\frac{1}{4}$ is called a **mixed number** because it is a *mixture* of a whole number and a fraction.

1. Write how many *whole* pies are shaded.

a)

    _2_ whole pies

b)

    _____ whole pie

c)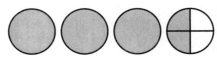

    _____ whole pies

2. Write a *mixed number* for the picture.

a)  $2\frac{1}{4}$

b)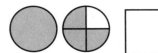

c)

d)

e)

3. Shade the amount of pie given in the mixed number. There may be more pies than you need.

a) $2\frac{1}{2}$

b) $1\frac{1}{4}$

c) $2\frac{3}{4}$

d) $3\frac{1}{3}$

4. In Question 5, you will draw a picture of $2\frac{1}{4}$ pies.

   a) How many fully shaded pies will there be?

   b) How many partly shaded pies will there be?

   c) How many equal parts will the partly shaded pie be divided into? Explain.

   d) How many of the equal parts will be shaded?

5. Sketch pies for the mixed number.

   a) $2\frac{1}{4}$ pies   b) $3\frac{3}{4}$ pies   c) $2\frac{3}{6}$ pies   d) $1\frac{6}{8}$ pies

Jessica and her friends ate 5 quarter-sized pieces of pizza.

Altogether they ate $\frac{5}{4}$ pizzas.

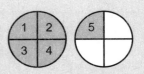

When the numerator is larger than the denominator, the fraction represents *more than* a whole. These are called **improper fractions**. They include fractions that represent a whole. Example: $\frac{3}{3}$.

6. Describe the shaded area as an *improper* fraction.

a)  $\boxed{\frac{5}{2}}$

b) 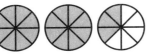 $\square$

c) 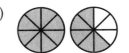 $\square$

d) 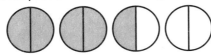 $\square$

e)  $\square$

f)  $\square$

7. Shade one piece at a time until you have shaded the given improper fraction.

a) $\frac{5}{2}$

b) $\frac{11}{4}$

c) $\frac{11}{3}$

d) $\frac{12}{4}$

8. Sketch pies for the improper fraction.

a) $\frac{4}{4}$ pies   b) $\frac{5}{4}$ pies   c) $\frac{6}{4}$ pies   d) $\frac{7}{4}$ pies

9. Write a mixed number and an improper fraction for the shaded amount.

a) $\boxed{2\frac{1}{2}}$ $\boxed{\frac{5}{2}}$

b) $\square$ $\square$

c) $\square$ $\square$

d) $\square$ $\square$

10. Sketch the pies. Then write an equivalent mixed number or improper fraction.

a) $2\frac{1}{2}$ pies   b) $\frac{9}{2}$ pies   c) $\frac{10}{4}$ pies   d) $3\frac{2}{3}$ pies

NS5-42 Mixed Numbers and Improper Fractions

How many half pieces are in 3 pies?

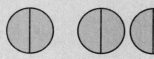

2 halves   3 × 2 halves = 6 halves

So there are 6 halves in 3 pies.

How many quarter pieces are in 3 pies?

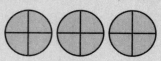

4 quarters   3 × 4 quarters = 12 quarters

So there are 12 quarters in 3 pies.

1. Find the number of halves, quarters, or thirds in the amount.

a) 1 pie = _____ halves

b) 2 pies = _____ halves

c) 3 pies = _____ halves

d) 1 pie = _____ quarters

e) 2 pies = _____ quarters

f) 3 pies = _____ quarters

g) 1 pie = __3__ thirds

h) 2 pies = _____ thirds

i) 3 pies = _____ thirds

How many halves are in $3\frac{1}{2}$ pies? Write the answer as an improper fraction.

2 halves   3 × 2 halves = 6 halves   6 halves + 1 more half = 7 halves

So there are 7 halves in $3\frac{1}{2}$ pies. So $3\frac{1}{2} = \frac{7}{2}$.

2. Find the number of halves, fourths, or thirds. Write the answer as an improper fraction.

a) $1\frac{1}{2}$ pies = __2__ halves + __1__ half = $\boxed{\frac{3}{2}}$

b) $2\frac{1}{2}$ pies = __4__ halves + __1__ half = $\boxed{\frac{5}{2}}$

c) $3\frac{1}{2}$ pies = ____ halves + ____ half = $\boxed{}$

d) $4\frac{1}{2}$ pies = ____ halves + ____ half = $\boxed{}$

e) $1\frac{1}{4}$ pies = ____ fourths + ____ fourth = $\boxed{}$

f) $1\frac{2}{4}$ pies = ____ fourths + ____ fourths = $\boxed{}$

g) $1\frac{3}{4}$ pie = ____ fourths + ____ fourths = $\boxed{}$

h) $2\frac{1}{4}$ pie = ____ fourths + ____ fourth = $\boxed{}$

i) $1\frac{1}{3}$ pies = ____ thirds + ____ third = $\boxed{}$

j) $1\frac{2}{3}$ pies = ____ thirds + ____ thirds = $\boxed{}$

3. Ella needs $3\frac{2}{3}$ cups of flour. Which scoop should she use? Explain.

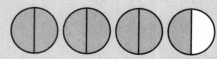

A $\frac{1}{3}$ B $\frac{1}{4}$

How many pies are there in $\frac{9}{4}$ pies?

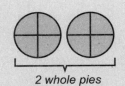 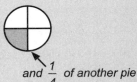

2 whole pies   and $\frac{1}{4}$ of another pie

There are 9 pieces altogether, and each pie has 4 pieces.

So you can find the number of pies by dividing 9 by 4: $9 \div 4 = 2$ Remainder 1

There are 2 whole pies with 1 quarter pie left over, so: $\frac{9}{4} = 2\frac{1}{4}$

4. Find the number of whole pies and the number of remaining pieces by dividing.

a) $\frac{6}{2}$ pies = ___3___ whole pies and ___0___ half pies = $\boxed{3}$ pies

b) $\frac{7}{2}$ pies = ___3___ whole pies and ___1___ half pie = $\boxed{3\frac{1}{2}}$ pies

c) $\frac{11}{4}$ pies = _____ whole pies and _____ quarter pies = $\boxed{}$ pies

d) $\frac{12}{4}$ pies = _____ whole pies and _____ quarter pies = $\boxed{}$ pies

5. Write the improper fraction as a mixed number by dividing.

a) $\frac{6}{2}$ $6 \div 2 =$ _3_ R _0_

So $\frac{6}{2} = \boxed{3}$

b) $\frac{7}{2}$ $7 \div 2 =$ _3_ R _1_

So $\frac{7}{2} = \boxed{3\frac{1}{2}}$

c) $\frac{7}{4}$ $7 \div 4 =$ ___ R ____

So $\frac{7}{4} = \boxed{}$

d) $\frac{8}{4}$ e) $\frac{10}{3}$ f) $\frac{11}{3}$

6. Circle the greater mixed number or improper fraction.

a) $8\frac{2}{5}$ $8\frac{4}{5}$ b) $\frac{18}{7}$ $\frac{16}{7}$ c) $19\frac{7}{8}$ $30\frac{1}{8}$ **BONUS ▶** $\frac{1285}{36}$ $\frac{1582}{36}$

7. Order the mixed numbers or improper fractions as indicated.

a) $\frac{22}{3}$ $\frac{8}{3}$ $\frac{12}{3}$ $\frac{34}{3}$

$\boxed{} < \boxed{} < \boxed{} < \boxed{}$

b) $5\frac{4}{5}$ $3\frac{4}{5}$ $6\frac{1}{5}$ $3\frac{2}{5}$

$\boxed{} > \boxed{} > \boxed{} > \boxed{}$

NS5-43 Fractions of Whole Numbers

Don has 6 cookies.

He wants to give $\frac{1}{3}$ of his cookies to a friend.

He makes 3 equal groups and gives 1 group to his friend.

There are 2 cookies in each group, so $\frac{1}{3}$ of 6 is 2.

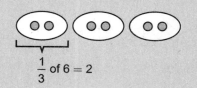

$\frac{1}{3}$ of 6 = 2

1. Use the picture to find the fraction of the number.

a)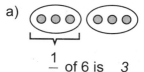

$\frac{1}{2}$ of 6 is __3__

b)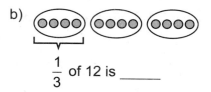

$\frac{1}{3}$ of 12 is _____

c)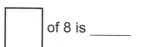

☐ of 8 is _____

d)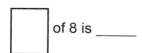

☐ of 8 is _____

Tina has 10 cookies. She wants to give $\frac{2}{5}$ of her cookies to a friend. She makes 5 equal groups and gives 2 of the groups to her friend.

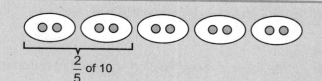

$\frac{2}{5}$ of 10

There are 2 in each group. So there are 4 in 2 groups. So $\frac{2}{5}$ of 10 is 4.

2. Circle the given amount.

a) $\frac{2}{3}$ of 6

b) $\frac{4}{4}$ of 8

c) $\frac{3}{5}$ of 10

d) $\frac{3}{4}$ of 12

3. Draw the correct number of dots in each group, then circle the given amount.

a) $\frac{2}{3}$ of 12   ◯ ◯ ◯

b) $\frac{2}{3}$ of 9   ◯ ◯ ◯

4. Draw a picture to find $\frac{3}{4}$ of 16 cookies.

Tristan finds $\frac{1}{3}$ of 6 by dividing: 6 divided into 3 equal groups is 2 in each group.

$6 \div 3 = 2$ So $\frac{1}{3}$ of 6 is 2.

5. Find the fraction of the number. Write the division you used in the box.

a) $\frac{1}{2}$ of 8 = __4__

$$8 \div 2$$

b) $\frac{1}{2}$ of 10 = _____

c) $\frac{1}{2}$ of 14 = _____

d) $\frac{1}{2}$ of 30 = _____

e) $\frac{1}{3}$ of 9 = _____

f) $\frac{1}{3}$ of 15 = _____

BONUS▶ $\frac{1}{10\,000}$ of 50 000 = _____

6. Circle $\frac{1}{2}$ of the set of lines. Hint: Count the lines and divide by 2.

a) | | | | | |

b) | | | | | | | | | |

c) | | | | | | | | | | | |

d) | | | | | | | | | | | | | |

7. Shade $\frac{1}{3}$ of the circles. Then circle $\frac{2}{3}$.

a)

b) ○○○○○○○○○○○○

c) ○○○

d) ○○○○○○○
○○○○○○

8. Shade $\frac{1}{4}$ of the triangles. Then circle $\frac{2}{4}$.

9. Shade $\frac{4}{5}$ of the boxes. Hint: First count the boxes and find $\frac{1}{5}$.

a)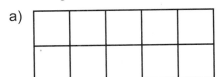

b)

NS5-44 Fractions and Word Problems

1. The chart shows the times of day when a lizard is active.

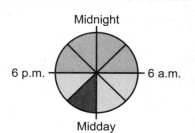

☐ awake but inactive
■ asleep
☐ awake and active

What fraction of the day is the lizard …

a) awake but inactive?   b) asleep?   c) awake and active?

2. Describe the set of letters in at least three ways using the fraction $\frac{3}{6}$.

b A N A n a

3. Use each fraction twice to describe the set of shapes: $\frac{1}{7}$, $\frac{3}{7}$, $\frac{4}{7}$.

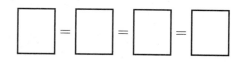

4. Write four equivalent fractions for the amount shaded in the picture.

$\boxed{} = \boxed{} = \boxed{} = \boxed{}$

5. Anna's backpack weighs $\frac{3}{4}$ kg. Raj's backpack weighs $\frac{1}{2}$ kg. Whose backpack weighs less, Anna's or Raj's?

6. A salmon is $\frac{3}{5}$ m long and a tuna is $\frac{3}{7}$ m long. Which fish is longer? Explain how you know.

BONUS ▶ Josh biked $\frac{10}{50}$ km in one minute. Mary biked $\frac{10}{40}$ km in one minute. Who cycled farther in one minute? Who cycled faster? Explain.

NS5-45 Multiplicative Relationships and Times as Many

1. What is being compared?

   a) Sean drives at 45 km/h.

   _____ and _____

   b) Monica earns $8/h

   _____ and _____

   c) Use 2 eggs for 1 cup of flour.

   _____ and _____

2. Fill in the missing information.

   a) 1 book costs $4.

   2 books cost _____.

   3 books cost _____.

   4 books cost _____.

   b) 1 ticket costs $6.

   2 tickets cost _____.

   3 tickets cost _____.

   4 tickets cost _____.

   c) 1 apple costs 20¢.

   2 apples cost _____.

   3 apples cost _____.

   4 apples cost _____.

   d) 30 km in 1 hour

   _____ km in 2 hours

   _____ km in 3 hours

   _____ km in 4 hours

   e) $12 allowance in 1 week

   _____ allowance in 2 weeks

   _____ allowance in 3 weeks

   _____ allowance in 4 weeks

   f) 1 teacher for 25 students

   2 teachers for _____ students

   3 teachers for _____ students

   4 teachers for _____ students

   g) 10 cups of water for 1 kg of rice

   _____ cups of water for 5 kg of rice

3. Multiply to find the missing information.

   a) ┌── 1 book costs $5 ──┐
      │×3   │×3
      └→ 3 books cost _$15_ ←┘

   b) 2 km in 1 hour

   _____ km in 6 hours

   c) 1 box for 6 markers

   5 boxes for _____ markers

   d) 1 magazine costs $7

   4 magazines cost _____

   e) 1 ticket costs $11

   _____ tickets cost $44

   f) 1 table for 5 students

   8 tables for _____ students

4. Edmond drives 100 km in one hour. How many kilometres will he drive in 7 hours? _____

5. Kathy reads 8 pages in one day. How many pages will she read in 7 days? _____

6. Find the missing information.

   a) 2 books cost $10.

   4 books cost _$20_.

   b) 4 mangoes cost $12.

   2 mangoes cost _____.

   c) 6 cans of juice cost $9.

   24 cans of juice cost _____.

7. Shade half of the circle. How many parts did you shade?

a) $\frac{1}{2}$ of 4

I shaded __2__ parts.

So $\frac{1}{2}$ as many as 4 is __2__.

b) $\frac{1}{2}$ of 8

I shaded _____ parts.

So $\frac{1}{2}$ as many as 8 is _____.

c) $\frac{1}{2}$ of 6

I shaded _____ parts.

So $\frac{1}{2}$ as many as 6 is _____.

BONUS ▶ $\frac{1}{2}$ of 10

I shaded _____ parts.

So $\frac{1}{2}$ as many as 10 is _____.

8. Shade a whole circle and half of the next circle.

a) $1\frac{1}{2}$ of 4

I shaded __6__ parts.

So $1\frac{1}{2}$ of 4 is __6__.

I shaded $\boxed{1\frac{1}{2}}$ times as many as 4.

b) $1\frac{1}{2}$ of 8

I shaded _____ parts.

So $1\frac{1}{2}$ of 8 is _____.

I shaded $\boxed{}$ times as many as 8.

c) $1\frac{1}{2}$ of 6

I shaded _____ parts.

So $1\frac{1}{2}$ of 6 is _____.

I shaded $\boxed{}$ times as many as 6.

BONUS ▶ $1\frac{1}{2}$ of 10

I shaded _____ parts.

So $1\frac{1}{2}$ of 10 is _____.

I shaded $\boxed{}$ times as many as 10.

9. Evan answers 10 questions in one hour.

a) How many questions does he answer in 2 hours? _____

b) How many questions in half an hour? _____

c) How many questions in $2\frac{1}{2}$ hours? _____

NS5-46 Decimal Tenths and Hundredths

A **tenth** (or $\frac{1}{10}$) can be represented in different ways.

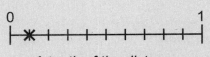

A tenth of the distance between 0 and 1

A tenth of a pie

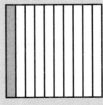

A tenth of hundreds block

A tenth of tens block

Tenths commonly appear in units of measurement. Example: a millimetre is a tenth of a centimetre

Mathematicians invented decimal tenths as a short form for tenths: $\frac{1}{10} = 0.1$, $\frac{2}{10} = 0.2$, and so on.

1. Write a fraction and a decimal for the shaded part in the boxes below.

a) 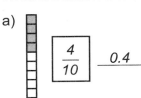 $\frac{4}{10}$ 0.4

b) 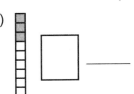   ☐ ____

c) 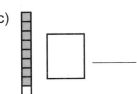   ☐ ____

d) 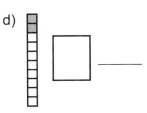   ☐ ____

2. Write the decimal.

a) 5 tenths = _0.5_   b) 4 tenths = _____   c) 6 tenths = _____   d) 9 tenths = _____

3. Shade to show the decimal.

a) 0.3   b) 0.8   c) 0.1   d) 0.4

4. Show the decimal on the number line.

a) 0.8 of the distance from 0 to 1

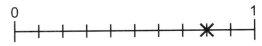

b) 0.2 of the distance from 0 to 1

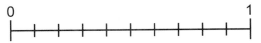

c) 0.5 of the distance from 0 to 1

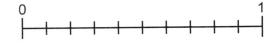

d) 0.7 of the distance from 0 to 1

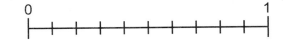

A **hundredth** (or $\frac{1}{100}$) can be represented in different ways.

A hundredth of a hundreds block

0   1

A hundredth of the distance from 0 to 1

Mathematicians invented decimal hundredths as a short form for hundredths.

Examples: $\frac{1}{100} = 0.01$, $\frac{8}{100} = 0.08$, $\frac{37}{100} = 0.37$

5. Write a fraction for the shaded part of the hundreds block. Then write the fraction as a decimal.
Hint: Count by 10s for each column or row that is shaded.

a)  $\frac{67}{100} = 0.67$

b)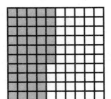

c)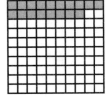

d)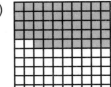

e)

BONUS ▶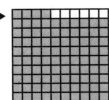

6. Write the decimal.

a) 18 hundredths = _____

b) 9 hundredths = _____

c) 90 hundredths = _____

REMINDER ▶ Points farther to the right on a number line represent greater numbers.

Example: 5 is to the right of 3 because 5 > 3.

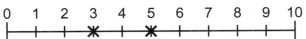

---

7. a) Show the decimals on the number line.

A. 0.24   **B.** 0.70   **C.** 0.06   **D.** 0.45

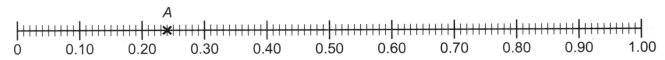

b) Write the decimals in part a) from least to greatest.

_____ < _____ < _____ < _____

1. Shade the same amount in the second square. Then count by 10s to find the number of hundredths. Write your answer as a fraction and a decimal.

a)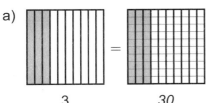

$$\frac{3}{10} = \frac{30}{100}$$

0.3 = ___0.30___

b)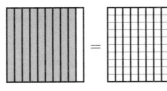

$$\frac{9}{10} = \frac{}{100}$$

0.9 = _____

c)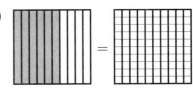

$$\frac{6}{10} = \frac{}{100}$$

0.6 = _____

2. a) Complete the table.

	Fraction Tenths	Fraction Hundredths	Picture	Decimal Tenths	Decimal Hundredths
i)	$\frac{2}{10}$	$\frac{20}{100}$		0.2	0.20
ii)					
iii)					

b) Use part a) to write the decimals from least to greatest: 0.40   0.2   0.7

_____ < _____ < _____

3. Write how many tenths and how many hundredths. Then write an equation with decimals.

A. _____ tenths

= _____ hundredths

So _____ = _____

B. _____ tenths

= _____ hundredths

So _____ = _____

C. _____ tenths

= _____ hundredths

So _____ = _____

4. Show the decimals on the number line. Then write the decimals from least to greatest.

a) **A.** 0.40   **B.** 0.05   **C.** 0.27

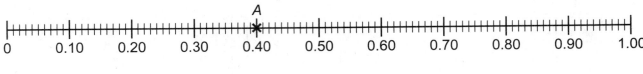

_____ < _____ < _____

b) **A.** 0.80   **B.** 0.08   **C.** 0.05

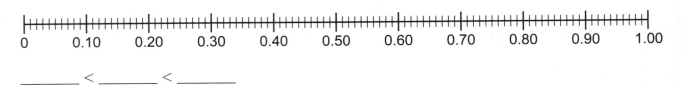

_____ < _____ < _____

5. Write the decimal as a fraction with denominator 100.

a) $0.7 = \dfrac{}{10} = \dfrac{}{100}$ b) $0.48 = \dfrac{}{100}$ c) $0.09 = \dfrac{}{100}$ d) $0.3 = \boxed{}$

6. Write the fraction as a decimal with 2 digits after the decimal point.

a) $\dfrac{6}{10} = 0.\underline{}$ b) $\dfrac{77}{100} = 0.\underline{}\,\underline{}$ c) $\dfrac{5}{10} = 0.\underline{}$ d) $\dfrac{9}{100} = 0.\underline{}\,\underline{}$

$= 0.\underline{}\,\underline{}$ $= 0.\underline{}\,\underline{}$

7. Cross out the equalities that are incorrect.

$0.52 = \dfrac{52}{100}$ $0.8 = \dfrac{8}{10}$ $\dfrac{17}{100} = 0.17$ $\dfrac{3}{100} = 0.03$

$0.7 = \dfrac{7}{100}$ $0.53 = \dfrac{53}{100}$ $0.05 = \dfrac{5}{100}$ $0.02 = \dfrac{2}{10}$

8. Write the decimals as hundredths to compare the decimals. Then write < or > in the box.

a) 0.4   0.73   b) 0.2   0.16   c) 0.7   0.59

$= \dfrac{}{100}$ $= \dfrac{}{100}$ $= \dfrac{}{}$ $= \dfrac{}{}$ $= \dfrac{}{}$ $= \dfrac{}{}$

0.4 $\boxed{}$ 0.73   0.2 $\boxed{}$ 0.16   0.7 $\boxed{}$ 0.59

NS5-48 Combining Tenths and Hundredths

1. Describe the shaded part of the hundreds block in four ways.

a)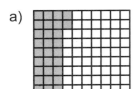

      _32_ hundredths = _3_ tenths _2_ hundredths

$$\frac{32}{100} = 0.\underline{\ 3\ }\ \underline{\ 2\ }$$

b)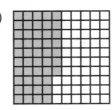

      ___ hundredths = ___ tenths ___ hundredths

$$\frac{\quad}{100} = 0.\underline{\quad}\ \underline{\quad}$$

c)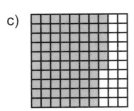

      ___ hundredths = ___ tenths ___ hundredths

$$\frac{\quad}{100} = 0.\underline{\quad}\ \underline{\quad}$$

d)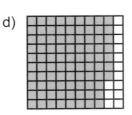

      ___ hundredths = ___ tenths ___ hundredths

$$\frac{\quad}{100} = 0.\underline{\quad}\ \underline{\quad}$$

2. Fill in the blanks.

a) 71 hundredths = _7_ tenths _1_ hundredth

$$\frac{71}{100} = 0.\underline{\ 7\ }\ \underline{\ 1\ }$$

b) 28 hundredths = ____ tenths ____ hundredths

$$\frac{\quad}{100} = 0.\underline{\quad}\ \underline{\quad}$$

c) 41 hundredths = ___ tenths ___ hundredth

$$\frac{\quad}{100} = 0.\underline{\quad}\ \underline{\quad}$$

d) 60 hundredths = ___ tenths ___ hundredths

$$\frac{\quad}{100} = 0.\underline{\quad}\ \underline{\quad}$$

e) 6 hundredths = ___ tenths ___ hundredths

$$\frac{\quad}{100} = 0.\underline{\quad}\ \underline{\quad}$$

f) 95 hundredths = ___ tenths ___ hundredths

$$\frac{\quad}{100} = 0.\underline{\quad}\ \underline{\quad}$$

3. Describe the decimal in two ways.

a) 0.52 = _5_ tenths _2_ hundredths

      = _52 hundredths_

b) 0.11 = ___ tenth ___ hundredth

      = _____

c) 0.70 = ___ tenths ___ hundredths

      = _____

d) 0.07 = ___ tenths ___ hundredths

      = _____

Jasmin describes the distance covered on a number line in two ways.

43 hundredths = 4 tenths 3 hundredths

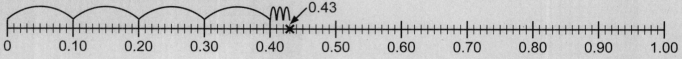

4. Write the distance covered in two ways.

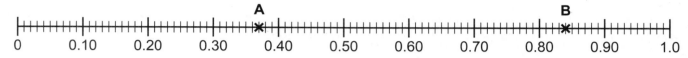

A. ____ tenths ____ hundredths

= ____ hundredths

B. ____ tenths ____ hundredths

= ____ hundredths

5. Estimate and mark the location of the decimals on the number line.

a) **A.** 0.62   **B.** 0.35   **C.** 0.99   **D.** 0.05

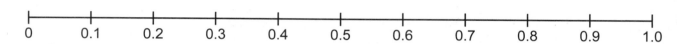

b) **A.** 0.37   **B.** 0.28   **C.** 0.51   **D.** 0.11

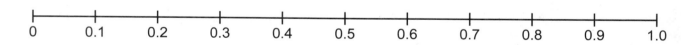

REMINDER ▶ A metre is 100 centimetres.

6. What part of a metre is the length shown? Write your answer as a decimal and a fraction.

a)

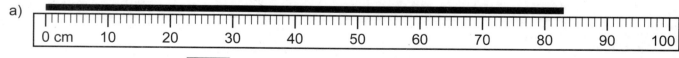

83 cm = ___0.83___ m = $\dfrac{83}{100}$ m

b)

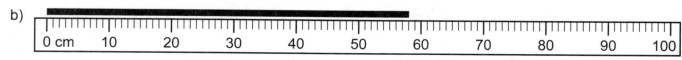

58 cm = _____ m = ☐ m

NS5-49 Decimals Greater Than 1

A mixed number can be written as a decimal.

Examples: $12\dfrac{3}{10} = 12.3$ $2\dfrac{85}{100} = 2.85$

The decimal point separates the whole number part (on the left) from the fraction part (on the right).

1. Write the mixed number as a decimal.

a) $3\dfrac{4}{10} = $ _____

b) $12\dfrac{5}{10} = $ _____

c) $8\dfrac{45}{100} = $ _____

d) $46\dfrac{3}{100} = $ _____

REMINDER ▶

The number of digits to the right of the decimal point = the number of zeros in the denominator.

Examples: $3.\textbf{50} = 3\dfrac{50}{100}$ $3.\textbf{5} = 3\dfrac{5}{10}$ $3.\textbf{05} = 3\dfrac{5}{100}$

2. Write the denominator of the fraction part for the equivalent mixed number.

a) 4.9 _____

b) 1.58 _____

c) 15.08 _____

BONUS ▶ 18.40 _____

3. Write the decimal as a mixed number.

a) 3.81 =

b) 6.9 =

c) 7.04 =

d) 18.15 =

e) 13.4 =

f) 17.06 =

g) 193.45 =

BONUS ▶ 1007.04 =

You can write a decimal in words. Use "and" for the decimal point.

Examples: $12\dfrac{3}{10} = 12.3 = $ twelve **and** three tenths $2\dfrac{85}{100} = 2.85 = $ two **and** eighty-five hundredths

4. Write "tenths" or "hundredths." Hint: Count the digits to the right of the decimal point.

a) 3.12 = three and twelve _____

b) 18.7 = eighteen and seven _____

c) 6.05 = six and five _____

d) 20.8 = twenty and eight _____

5. Write the equivalent words or decimal.

a) 7.4 = _____

b) 4.09 = _____

c) seventy-four and eleven hundredths = _____

d) twenty and four tenths = _____

REMINDER ▶ You can change an improper fraction to a mixed number by dividing.

Example: $\frac{28}{10}$ $28 \div 10 = 2$ R 8, so $\frac{28}{10} = 2\frac{8}{10}$

6. Change the improper fraction to a mixed number.

a) $\frac{74}{10}$ $74 \div 10 = $ _____ R _____

     So $\frac{74}{10} = $

b) $\frac{625}{100}$ $625 \div 100 = $ _____ R _____

     So $\frac{625}{100} = $

7. Change the improper fraction to a mixed number and then to a decimal.

a) $\frac{35}{10} = 3\frac{5}{10} = 3.5$

b) $\frac{387}{100} = 3\frac{87}{100} = 3.87$

c) $\frac{41}{10} = $

d) $\frac{642}{100} = $

e) $\frac{564}{100} = $

f) $\frac{808}{100} = $

8. Write the decimal as an improper fraction with denominator 10 or 100.

a) $3.8 = $ b) $7.08 = $ c) $8.60 = $ d) $60.04 = $

e) $70.8 = $ f) $17.5 = $ g) $31.89 = $ h) $90.4 = $

Remember: $\frac{8}{10} = \frac{80}{100}$ So $2\frac{8}{10} = 2\frac{80}{100}$ So $2.8 = 2.80$

9. Complete the table.

	Decimal Tenths	Fraction Tenths	Fraction Hundredths	Decimal Hundredths
a)	2.7	$\frac{27}{10}$	$\frac{270}{100}$	2.70
b)	3.8			
c)	3.9			
d)	6.4			

	Decimal Tenths	Fraction Tenths	Fraction Hundredths	Decimal Hundredths
e)	59.4			
f)		$\frac{75}{10}$		
g)			$\frac{670}{100}$	
h)				30.80

NS5-50 Decimal Fractions and Place Value

Decimals are a way to record place values based on decimal fractions.

decimal point

5 thousands → **5342.67** ← 7 hundredths

3 hundreds   4 tens   2 ones   6 tenths

1. Write the place value of the underlined digit.

   a) 2.7 _____ones_____

   b) 53.9 _____

   c) 107.1 _____

   d) 236.4 _____

   e) 501.08 _____

   f) 734.58 _____

2. Write the place value of the digit 3 in the number. Hint: First underline the 3 in the number.

   a) 261.93 _____

   b) 405.03 _____

   c) 7103.8 _____

   d) 3.02 _____

   e) 3919.1 _____

   f) 2854.30 _____

You can also write numbers using a place value chart. Example:

This is the number 7102.85 in a place value chart:

Thousands	Hundreds	Tens	Ones	Tenths	Hundredths
7	1	0	2	8	5

3. Write the number into the place value chart.

		Thousands	Hundreds	Tens	Ones	Tenths	Hundredths
a)	5227.60	5	2	2	7	6	0
b)	853.4						
c)	0.05						
d)	27.00						
e)	4.58						

4. What is the value of the digit 9 in each decimal? Write the answer two ways.

   a) 0.49 $\frac{9}{100}$ or 9 _____hundredths_____

   b) 3.92 $\frac{9}{}$ or 9 _____

   c) 8.90 $\frac{9}{}$ or 9 _____

   d) 3.09 $\frac{9}{}$ or 9 _____

5. Put a decimal point in the number so that the digit 4 has the value $\frac{4}{10}$.

   a) 6 4 1

   b) 1 0 4

   c) 1 3 4 2

   BONUS ▶ 1 0 0 0 1 4

NS5-51 Thousandths

	1 one	1 tenth	1 hundredth	1 thousandth
	$\frac{1}{1} = 1$	$\frac{1}{10} = 0.1$	$\frac{1}{100} = 0.01$	$\frac{1}{1000} = 0.001$

1. Complete the table.

	Fraction Tenths	Fraction Hundredths	Fraction Thousandths	Decimal Tenths	Decimal Hundredths	Decimal Thousandths
a)	$\frac{6}{10}$	$\frac{60}{100}$	$\frac{600}{1000}$	0.6	0.60	0.600
b)				0.3		
c)		$\frac{80}{100}$				
d)						0.500
e)	$\frac{4}{10}$					
f)			$\frac{200}{1000}$			
g)					0.70	

2. Write the fraction as a decimal with three digits after the decimal point.

a) $\frac{2}{10} = \underline{0} . \underline{2} \ \underline{0} \ \underline{0}$ b) $\frac{74}{100} = \underline{\ } . \underline{\ } \ \underline{\ } \ \underline{\ }$ c) $\frac{9}{1000} = \underline{\ } . \underline{\ } \ \underline{\ } \ \underline{\ }$

d) $\frac{101}{1000} = \underline{\ } . \underline{\ } \ \underline{\ } \ \underline{\ }$ e) $\frac{596}{1000} = \underline{\ } . \underline{\ } \ \underline{\ } \ \underline{\ }$ f) $\frac{110}{1000} = \underline{\ } . \underline{\ } \ \underline{\ } \ \underline{\ }$

g) $\frac{9}{10} = \underline{\ } . \underline{\ } \ \underline{\ } \ \underline{\ }$ h) $\frac{1}{100} = \underline{\ } . \underline{\ } \ \underline{\ } \ \underline{\ }$ i) $\frac{10}{100} = \underline{\ } . \underline{\ } \ \underline{\ } \ \underline{\ }$

3. Write the decimal as a fraction with denominator 1000.

a) $0.346 = \frac{}{1000}$ b) $0.27 = \frac{}{1000}$ c) $0.8 = \frac{}{1000}$ d) $0.101 = \frac{}{1000}$

e) $0.05 = \frac{}{1000}$ f) $0.003 = \frac{}{1000}$ g) $0.704 = \frac{}{1000}$ h) $0.060 = \frac{}{1000}$

NS5-52 Comparing and Ordering Decimal Fractions and Decimals

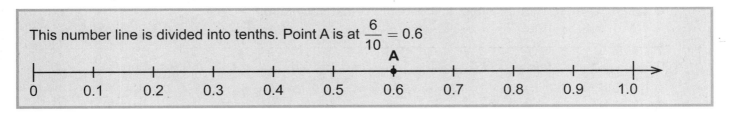

This number line is divided into tenths. Point A is at $\frac{6}{10} = 0.6$

1. Write a decimal and a fraction for each point on the number line.

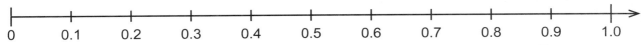

	A	B	C	D
Decimal	0.1			
Fraction	$\frac{1}{10}$			

2. Mark the decimal or fraction on the number line with a dot and a letter.

A. 0.3 **B.** 0.2 **C.** 0.4 **D.** $\frac{7}{10}$

E. $\frac{9}{10}$ **F.** $\frac{6}{10}$ **G.** 0.1 **BONUS ▶ H.** $\frac{99}{100}$

This number line is divided into hundredths. Point A is at $\frac{28}{100} = 0.28$

3. Write a fraction and a decimal for each point on the number line.

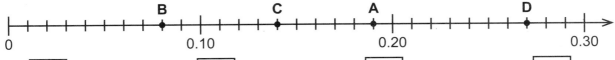

A. ☐ _____ **B.** ☐ _____ **C.** ☐ _____ **D.** ☐ _____

4. Mark the decimal or fraction on the number line with a dot and a letter.

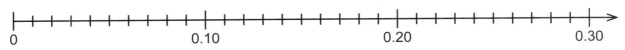

A. 0.13 **B.** $\frac{1}{100}$ **C.** 0.04 **D.** $\frac{17}{100}$

5. a) Estimate the position of the decimal or fraction on the number line by marking a dot and a letter. Hint: Change all the fractions into decimals.

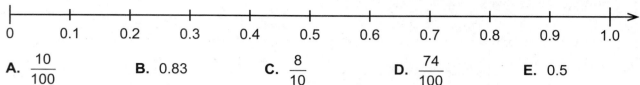

A. $\frac{10}{100}$ **B.** 0.83 **C.** $\frac{8}{10}$ **D.** $\frac{74}{100}$ **E.** 0.5

_____0.10_____ _____ _____ _____ _____

b) Order $\frac{10}{100}$, $\frac{8}{10}$, and 0.5 from least to greatest. _____ < _____ < _____

6. Change all decimals to fractions with denominator 100. Write the fractions in order from greatest to least.

a) $\frac{27}{100}$ 0.9   0.25

| $\frac{27}{100}$ | $\frac{90}{100}$ | $\frac{25}{100}$ |

| $\frac{90}{100}$ > | $\frac{27}{100}$ > | $\frac{25}{100}$ |

b) 0.2   0.8   0.35

☐ ☐ ☐

☐ > ☐ > ☐

c) 0.3 $\frac{22}{100}$ $\frac{39}{100}$

☐ ☐ ☐

☐ > ☐ > ☐

d) 0.45 $\frac{47}{100}$ 0.4

☐ ☐ ☐

☐ > ☐ > ☐

e) 0.08 $\frac{7}{100}$ 0.1

☐ ☐ ☐

☐ > ☐ > ☐

f) 0.24 $\frac{4}{10}$ $\frac{20}{100}$

☐ ☐ ☐

☐ > ☐ > ☐

7. Use the numbers 10 and 100 as denominators to make the statement true.

a) $\frac{6}{10} > \frac{6}{100}$

b) $\frac{6}{\rule{1cm}{0.4pt}} < \frac{6}{\rule{1cm}{0.4pt}}$

BONUS ▶ $\frac{7}{\rule{1cm}{0.4pt}} < \frac{6}{\rule{1cm}{0.4pt}}$

8. Use the numbers 5 and 60 as numerators to make the statement true.

a) $\frac{5}{100} < \frac{60}{100}$

b) $\frac{\rule{1cm}{0.4pt}}{10} < \frac{\rule{1cm}{0.4pt}}{100}$

9. a) Cam thinks $\frac{3}{10}$ is less than 0.30 because 3 is less than 30. Do you agree? Explain.

b) Lily thinks 0.1 is less than $\frac{8}{100}$ because 8 is greater than 1. Do you agree? Explain.

NS5-53 Comparing and Ordering Fractions and Decimals

1.

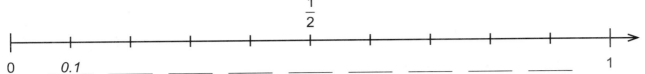

$\frac{1}{2}$

0   0.1   ____   ____   ____   ____   ____   ____   ____   ____   1

a) Write a decimal for each mark on the number line above.

b) Which decimal is equal to one half? $\frac{1}{2}$ = _____

c) Use the number line above to compare the pair of numbers. Write <, >, or = in the box.

i) 0.7 ⬚> $\frac{1}{2}$ ii) $\frac{1}{2}$ ⬚ 0.6   iii) $\frac{1}{2}$ ⬚ 0.4

iv) $\frac{1}{2}$ ⬚ 0.5   v) 0.1 ⬚ $\frac{1}{2}$ vi) 0.2 ⬚ $\frac{1}{2}$

2. Use the number lines to compare the pair of numbers. Write <, >, or = in the box.

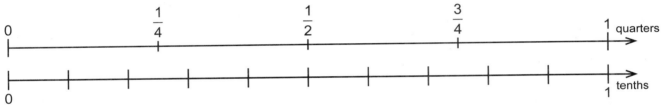

a) 0.8 ⬚ $\frac{3}{4}$ b) 0.4 ⬚ $\frac{7}{10}$ c) $\frac{1}{4}$ ⬚ 0.4   d) 0.2 ⬚ $\frac{1}{4}$

e) 0.5 ⬚ $\frac{1}{2}$ f) 0.3 ⬚ $\frac{1}{4}$ g) $\frac{3}{4}$ ⬚ 0.6   h) $\frac{3}{4}$ ⬚ 0.7

3. Use the number lines to compare the pair of numbers. Write <, >, or = in the box.

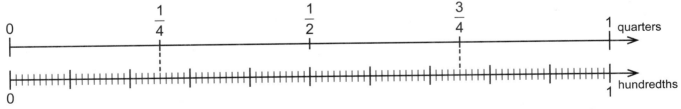

a) 0.21 ⬚ $\frac{1}{4}$ b) $\frac{1}{2}$ ⬚ 0.54   c) 0.75 ⬚ $\frac{3}{4}$ d) 0.26 ⬚ $\frac{1}{4}$

e) 0.74 ⬚ $\frac{3}{4}$ f) $\frac{1}{4}$ ⬚ 0.25   g) 0.50 ⬚ $\frac{1}{2}$ h) $\frac{3}{4}$ ⬚ 0.80

4. 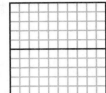 Shade $\frac{1}{2}$ of the squares. Write two fractions and two decimals for $\frac{1}{2}$.

Fractions: $\frac{1}{2}$ = $\frac{}{10}$ = $\frac{}{100}$

Decimals: $\frac{1}{2}$ = 0._____ = 0._____

5. Shade $\frac{1}{5}$ of the squares. Write two fractions and two decimals for $\frac{1}{5}$.

Fractions: $\frac{1}{5}$ = $\frac{}{10}$ = $\frac{}{100}$

Decimals: $\frac{1}{5}$ = 0._____ = 0._____

6. Write equivalent fractions.

a) $\frac{2}{5}$ = $\frac{}{10}$ = $\frac{}{100}$ b) $\frac{3}{5}$ = $\frac{}{10}$ = $\frac{}{100}$ c) $\frac{4}{5}$ = $\frac{}{10}$ = $\frac{}{100}$

7. Shade $\frac{1}{4}$ of the squares. Write a fraction and a decimal for $\frac{1}{4}$ and $\frac{3}{4}$.

Fractions: $\frac{1}{4}$ = $\frac{}{100}$ Fractions: $\frac{3}{4}$ = $\frac{}{100}$

Decimals: $\frac{1}{4}$ = 0._____   Decimals: $\frac{3}{4}$ = 0._____

8. Circle the greater number in the pair. Hint: First change all fractions and decimals to fractions with denominator 100.

a) $\frac{1}{2}$ 0.37

$\boxed{\frac{50}{100}}$ $\square$

b) $\frac{1}{4}$ 0.52

$\square$ $\square$

c) $\frac{2}{5}$ 0.42

$\square$ $\square$

d) 0.7 $\frac{3}{5}$

$\square$ $\square$

e) 0.23 $\frac{1}{5}$

$\square$ $\square$

f) 0.52 $\frac{1}{2}$

$\square$ $\square$

9. Write the numbers in order from least to greatest. Explain how you found your answer.

a) 0.7   0.32 $\frac{1}{2}$ b) $\frac{1}{4}$ $\frac{3}{5}$ 0.63   c) $\frac{2}{5}$ 0.35 $\frac{1}{2}$

NS5-54 Adding Decimals

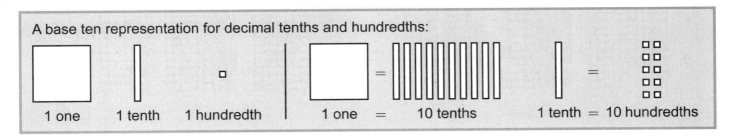

A base ten representation for decimal tenths and hundredths:

1 one   1 tenth   1 hundredth   1 one = 10 tenths   1 tenth = 10 hundredths

1. Regroup every 10 tenths as 1 one.

a)

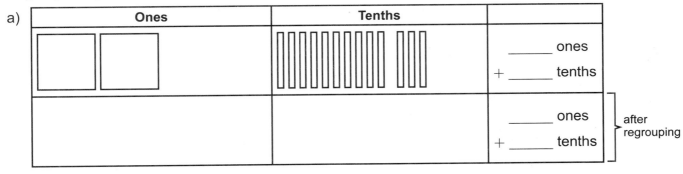

Ones	Tenths	
		_____ ones + _____ tenths
		_____ ones + _____ tenths after regrouping

b) 14 tenths = _____ one + _____ tenths   c) 23 tenths = _____ ones + _____ tenths

d) 49 tenths = _____ ones + _____ tenths   e) 67 tenths = _____ ones + _____ tenths

2. Regroup so that each place value has a single digit.

a) 3 ones + 12 tenths = __4__ ones + __2__ tenths

b) 7 tenths + 14 hundredths = _____ tenths + _____ hundredths

c) 8 tenths + 15 hundredths = _____ tenths + _____ hundredths

d) 6 tenths + 24 hundredths = _____ tenths + _____ hundredths

e) 1 tenth + 89 hundredths = _____ tenths + _____ hundredths

3. Regroup 1 tenth for 10 hundredths.

a) 4 tenths + 0 hundredths = __3__ tenths + __10__ hundredths

b) 8 tenths + 0 hundredths = _____ tenths + _____ hundredths

c) 4 tenths + 1 hundredth = _____ tenths + _____ hundredths

d) 6 tenths + 8 hundredths = _____ tenths + _____ hundredths

e) 1 tenth + 9 hundredths = _____ tenths + _____ hundredths

BONUS ▶ 1 tenth + 89 hundredths = _____ tenths + _____ hundredths

4. Write a decimal for each shaded part. Then add the decimals and shade your answer.

a)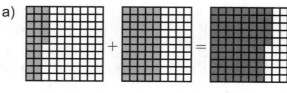

<u> 0.25 </u> + <u> 0.50 </u> = <u> 0.75 </u>

b)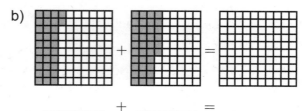

_____ + _____ = _____

c)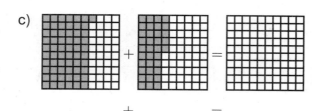

_____ + _____ = _____

d)

_____ + _____ = _____

e)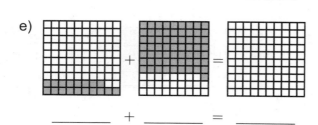

_____ + _____ = _____

BONUS ▶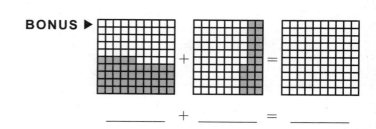

_____ + _____ = _____

5. Add by adding each place value.

a) $41.2 + 7.48$

Tens	Ones	Tenths	Hundredths
4	1	2	
+	7	4	8
4	8	6	8

b) $36.48 + 42.1$

Tens	Ones	Tenths	Hundredths
+			

6. Add by adding each place value. Then regroup.

a) $4.65 + 0.73$

Ones	Tenths	Hundredths
4	6	5
+ 0	7	3
4	13	8
5	3	8

← after regrouping →

b) $31.4 + 5.71$

Tens	Ones	Tenths	Hundredths
+			

7. Add the decimals by lining up the decimal points.

a) 0.41 + 0.37

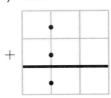

b) 0.52 + 0.46

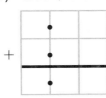

c) 0.05 + 0.83

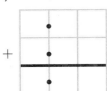

d) 0.4 + 0.04

You can show regrouping on a grid. Example: 4.8 + 3.5

8 tenths + 5 tenths = 13 tenths were regrouped as **1** one and **3** tenths

8. Add the decimals by lining up the decimal points. You will need to regroup.

a) 0.7 + 0.48

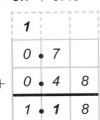

b) 0.26 + 0.65

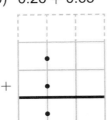

c) 0.63 + 0.84

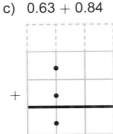

d) 0.17 + 0.43 + 1.32

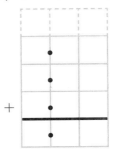

9. Add the decimals by lining up the decimal points. You may need to regroup.

a) 2.51 + 4.68

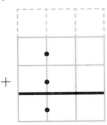

b) 5.45 + 3.45

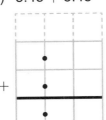

c) 8.48 + 0.09

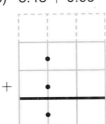

d) 0.87 + 0.04

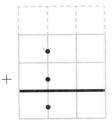

10. The mass of a dime is 1.75 g, and the mass of a quarter is 4.4 g. What is the total mass of one dime and two quarters?

11. Bill adds 21.4 + 4.21 on grid paper. He gets 63.5. What mistake did he make? Explain.

_____

_____

NS5-55 Adding Decimals and Subtracting Decimals

1. Subtract by crossing out the correct number of shaded boxes. Give the answer as a decimal.

a)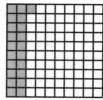

$0.21 - 0.11 =$ _____

b)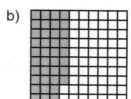

$0.38 - 0.12 =$ _____

c)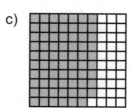

$0.69 - 0.34 =$ _____

d)

$0.57 - 0.25 =$ _____

2. Subtract the decimals by lining up the decimal points.

a) $0.74 - 0.31$

0	•	7	4
− 0	•	3	1
0	•	4	3

b) $0.65 - 0.24$

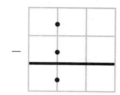

c) $3.47 - 2.2$

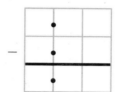

d) $6.49 - 0.35$

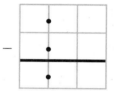

e) $2.51 - 1.51$

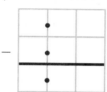

f) $3.79 - 2.06$

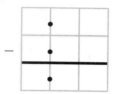

g) $8.84 - 7.10$

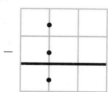

h) $5.19 - 3.07$

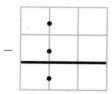

i) $4.08 - 4.04$

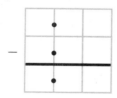

j) $2.15 - 2.03$

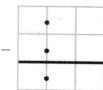

k) $5.52 - 2.41$

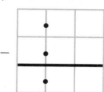

l) $9.83 - 2.70$

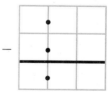

When subtracting decimals, you may have to regroup just like when you subtract whole numbers.

Example:

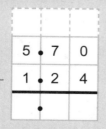

Regroup 1 tenth as 10 hundredths.

3. Subtract the decimals. Put a decimal point in your answer on the grid.

a) 0.81 − 0.58

```
        7   11
  0 . 8̶   1̶
− 0 . 5   8
───────────
  0 . 2   3
```

b) 5.72 − 3.56

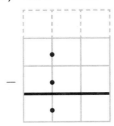

c) 6.15 − 4.2

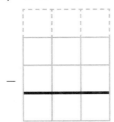

d) 2.46 − 0.38

e) 4.4 − 2.65

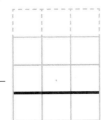

f) 31.1 − 22.2

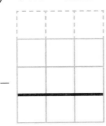

g) 7.45 − 6.68

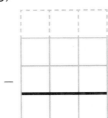

h) 5.20 − 1.23

4. Subtract the decimals on grid paper.

a) 0.87 − 0.26

b) 6.15 − 4.04

c) 5.83 − 3.69

5. Add or subtract mentally.

a) 0.54 + 0.31 = _____

b) 4.95 − 2.84 = _____

c) 7.09 − 4.02 = _____

d) 2.37 + 1.22 = _____

e) 5.73 − 1.62 = _____

f) 8.71 − 1.71 = _____

g) 1.45 + 2.54 = _____

h) 4.35 − 2.12 = _____

i) 9.47 − 7.46 = _____

6. What is the difference in the thickness of these coins?

a) a quarter (1.58 mm) and a dime (1.22 mm)

b) a nickel (1.76 mm) and a quarter (1.58 mm)

7. Sara made coloured water for a project by mixing 0.05 L of blue dye with 0.85 L of water. How many litres of blue-coloured water did she make?

8. An average house cat's body and head are about 0.46 m long. The tail is about 0.30 m long. What is the total length of an average house cat?

NS5-56 Dollar and Cent Notation

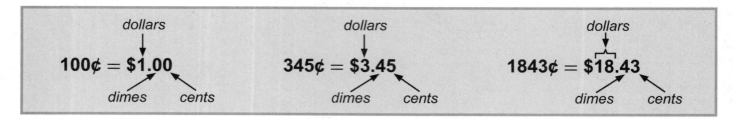

1. Write the amount in cent notation and then in dollar notation.

   a) 4 nickels = ___20¢___ = ___$0.20___

   b) 6 dimes = _____ = _____

   c) 1 quarter = _____ = _____

   d) 5 nickels = _____ = _____

   e) 3 quarters = _____ = _____

   f) 8 dimes = _____ = _____

   g) 1 loonie = _____ = _____

   h) 5 loonies = _____ = _____

   i) 7 loonies = _____ = _____

   j) 10 dimes = _____ = _____

   BONUS ▶

   k) 4 loonies, 3 dimes, and 1 nickel = _____ = _____

   l) 3 toonies, 2 loonies, 1 quarter, 1 dime, and 2 nickels = _____ = _____

2. Complete the table.

	Amount in ¢	Dollars	Dimes	Cents	Amount in $
a)	143¢	1	4	3	$1.43
b)	47¢	0			
c)	305¢				
d)	3¢				

   BONUS ▶

	Amount in ¢	Dollars	Dimes	Cents	Amount in $
	2016¢				

3. Write the amount in cent notation.

   a) $3.00 = ___300¢___

   b) $0.60 = _____

   c) $0.09 = _____

   d) $1.00 = _____

   e) $7.98 = _____

   f) $12.00 = _____

   g) $10.00 = _____

   h) $1.99 = _____

   i) $1.51 = _____

   j) $0.98 = _____

   k) $0.03 = _____

   l) $0.08 = _____

   m) $23.00 = _____

   n) $31.06 = _____

   o) $40.04 = _____

4. Write the amount in dollar notation.

a) 254¢ = ___$2.54___

b) 103¢ = _____

c) 216¢ = _____

d) 375¢ = _____

e) 300¢ = _____

f) 4¢ = _____

g) 607¢ = _____

h) 1908¢ = _____

i) 600¢ = _____

j) 99¢ = _____

k) 1200¢ = _____

BONUS ▶ 9008¢ = _____

5. Complete the table.

Dollars		Cents		Total
a)	 = ___$3___		= ___35¢___	___$3.35___
b)  	= _____		= _____	_____
c)  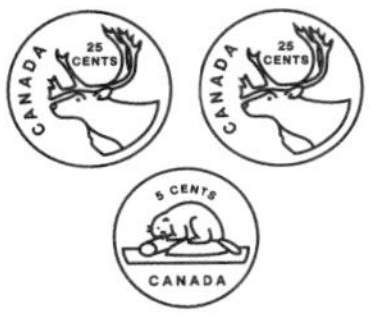	= _____		= _____	_____
d)  	= _____		= _____	_____
e)  	= _____		= _____	_____
f)  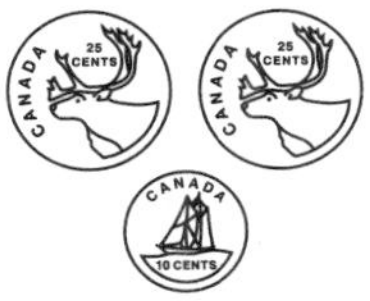	= _____		= _____	_____

6. Lela paid for a notebook with 3 coins. The notebook cost $6.00. Which coins did she use?

7. Show two ways to make $5.25 with 6 coins and/or bills.

8. Change the amount in dollar notation to cent notation. Then circle the greater amount.

   a) (175¢) or $1.73   b) $1.00 or 10¢   c) 6¢   or $0.04

                  173¢

   d) $5.98 or 597¢   e) 600¢ or $6.05   f) $0.87 or 187¢

9. Write each amount in cent notation. Then circle the greater amount of money in the pair.

   a) three dollars and sixty-five cents   or   three hundred fifty-six cents

      _____   _____

   b) nine dollars and twenty-eight cents   or   nine dollars and eighty-two cents

      _____   _____

   c) eight dollars and seventy-five cents   or $8.57

      _____   _____

10. Which is a greater amount of money: 168¢ or $1.65? Explain.

11. Marla has 1014¢, Ray has eleven dollars and forty-one cents, and Jessica has $11.04. Write Marla's amount and Ray's amount in dollar notation. Then order the three amounts from least to greatest.

   Marla's amount: 1014¢ = $_____

   Ray's amount: eleven dollars and forty-one cents = $_____

   _____ < _____ < _____

12. Sammy has 2308¢. Jacob has 2083¢. Write an amount in dollar notation that is …

   a) greater than both amounts. _____

   b) less than both amounts. _____

   c) between the two amounts. _____

1. Add.

a) $5.45 + $3.23

$	5	.	4	5
+ $	3	.	2	3
$		.		

b) $26.15 + $32.23

$		.		
+ $		.		
$		.		

c) $19.57 + $50.32

$		.		
+ $		.		
$		.		

2. Add. You will have to regroup.

a)

$	1	6	.	6	0
+ $	2	3	.	7	5
$			.		

b)

$	2	7	.	4	5
+ $	4	5	.	1	2
$			.		

c)

$	8	7	.	4	1
+ $		6	.	3	9
$			.		

d)

$	3	4	.	6	0
+ $	2	6	.	0	0
$			.		

e)

$	3	2	.	4	7
+ $	4	4	.	2	5
$			.		

f)

$	1	6	.	0	8
+ $	4	8	.	0	5
$			.		

3. Subtract. You will have to regroup.

a)

$	2	4	.	5	0
− $	2	1	.	7	5
$			.		

b)

$	3	6	.	4	5
− $	1	3	.	8	0
$			.		

c)

$	4	7	.	2	3
− $		6	.	7	2
$			.		

d)

$	5	3	.	0	4
− $	1	6	.	0	3
$			.		

e)

$	7	0	.	6	2
− $	2	5	.	5	1
$			.		

f)

$	8	4	.	1	7
− $	3	9	.	0	9
$			.		

4. Jasmin bought a pair of mittens for $7.25 and a T-shirt for $13.53. How much did Jasmin spend in total?

5. A library spent $270.25 on novels and $389.82 on movies and music. How much did the library spend in total?

6. Eric bought two baseball hats that cost $21.30 each. Add to find out how much he paid in total.

7. Raj has $25. If he buys a board game for $9.50 and a book for $10.35, will he have enough money left to buy a second book for $5.10?

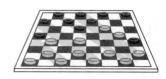

8. The regular price for a pair of glasses is $69.99. Today only, they are on sale for $10.50 off per pair. If Lynn buys her glasses today, how much will she pay?

BONUS ▶ If Lynn buys one pair of glasses today and one pair next week, how much will she pay in total?

9. Answer the question by looking at the items and their prices below.

a) If you bought a pair of shoes, a camera, and a water bottle, how much would you pay?

b) Which costs more: shoes and a soccer ball or pants?

c) Could you buy a water bottle, a hockey shirt, and shoes with $60? Explain how you found the answer.

d) What is the total cost of the three most expensive items?

BONUS ▶ How much would it cost to buy two pairs of pants? Explain how you could use a mental math strategy to simplify the calculation.

$28.50
$42.89
$49.95
$35.47
$12.30
$15.64

10. Try to find the answer mentally.

a) How much do 4 loaves of bread cost at $2.10 each?

b) Apples cost 50¢ each. How many could you buy with $3.00?

c) Permanent markers cost $3.10 each. How many could you buy if you had $12.00?

11. Sam spent $3.27 on apples, 563¢ on peaches, and four dollars and ninety-six cents on grapes. Write each amount in dollar notation. Use graph paper to find the total amount Sam spent.

NS5-58 Rounding Decimals

1. Draw an arrow to the 0 or to the 1 to show whether the circled decimal is closer to 0 or 1.

a)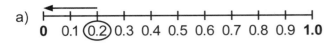

b)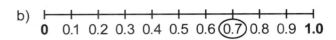

c)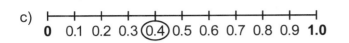

d)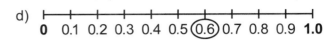

2. a) Which decimal numbers between 0 and 1.0 are closer to …

   i) 0? _____   ii) 1.0? _____

   b) Why is 0.5 a special case? _____

3. Draw an arrow to show which **whole number** you would round the circled number to.
   Then round to the nearest whole number.

a)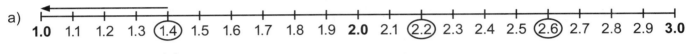

   Round to   _1.0_   _____   _____

b)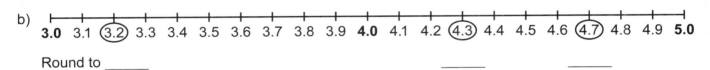

   Round to _____   _____   _____

4. If the statement is correct, write ✓ in the box. If the statement is not correct, write ✗ in the box.

   a) 3.6 is closer to 3.0 than to 4.0.   [✗]   b) 1.4 is closer to 1.0 than to 2.0.   [✓]

   c) 9.2 is closer to 10.0 than to 9.0. [ ]   d) 11.7 is closer to 11.0 than to 12.0. [ ]

   e) 25.6 is closer to 26.0 than to 25.0. [ ]   f) 111.7 is closer to 111.0 than to 112.0. [ ]

   g) 0.4 is closer to 1.0 than to 0. [ ]

   BONUS ▶
   1009.4 is closer to 1010.0 than to 1009.0. [ ]

5. Draw an arrow to show whether the circled number is closer to 0 or 1.00.

a)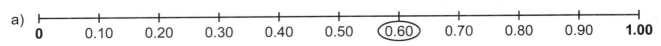

b)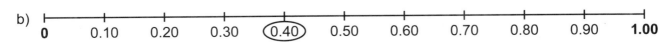

6. Draw an arrow to show whether the circled number is closer to 0 or 1.000.

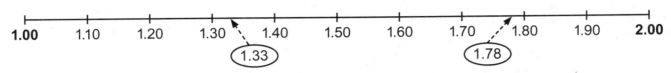

7. Draw an arrow to show which whole number you would round the circled number to.

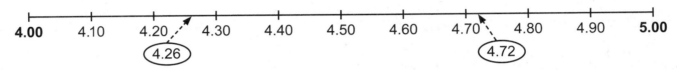

8. Draw an arrow to show which whole number you would round the circled number to.

REMINDER ▶ If the tenths digit in the decimal is …
0, 1, 2, 3, or 4 — you round *down*.   5, 6, 7, 8, or 9 — you round *up*.

9. Round to the nearest whole number.

a) 2.2 `2`

b) 2.6 `3`

c) 7.3 ☐

d) 5.8 ☐

e) 9.4 ☐

f) 8.5 ☐

g) 11.1 ☐

h) 30.7 ☐

i) 19.6 ☐

10. Round to the nearest tenth. Underline the tenths digit first. Then put your pencil on the digit to the right (the hundredths digit). This digit tells you whether to round up or down.

a) 1.4̲5 `1.5`

b) 1.83 ☐

c) 3.61 ☐

d) 3.42 ☐

e) 5.55 ☐

f) 6.67 ☐

g) 6.56 ☐

h) 8.47 ☐

i) 9.38 ☐

j) 7.94 ☐

k) 4.97 ☐

l) 9.96 ☐

11. A fish tank is 20.0 cm deep. It has a line marked on it at 19.6 cm.
The instructions say: CAUTION: DO NOT FILL ABOVE THIS LINE.

a) What is the nearest whole number to 19.6?

b) In this case, why would you not round 19.6 to the nearest whole number? Explain.

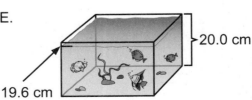

19.6 cm

20.0 cm

NS5-59 Estimating Sums and Differences for Decimals

Mathematicians use the symbol $\approx$ to mean "**approximately equal to.**"

1. Estimate the sum or difference using the whole-number parts of the decimal.
   Example: For **14**.35 + **0**.23 + **5**.74, estimate **14** + **0** + **5** = 19

   a) 3.9 + 4.25 $\approx$ ____ + ____ = ____   b) 7.03 − 5.42 $\approx$ ____ − ____ = ____

   c) 3.2 + 5.1 + 4.6 $\approx$ ____ + ____ + ____ = ____   d) 9.6 − 3.0 − 4.9 $\approx$ ____ − ____ − ____ = ____

2. Estimate by rounding to the nearest whole number. Then add or subtract.

   a)   3.2 | 3 | b)   1.6 | | c)   5.6 | | d)   6.8 | |
         + 1.3 + | 1 | + 0.6 + | | − 3.1 − | | − 0.5 − | |
         _____   _____   _____   _____
              4

   e)   1.9 | | f)   0.4 | | g)   8.6 | | h)   29.8 | |
         + 0.8 + | | − 0.2 − | | + 1.1 + | | + 68.9 + | |
         _____   _____   _____   _____

   i) 0.6 + 0.3   j) 0.9 − 0.4   k) 2.6 + 0.5   l) 3.5 − 0.5

   m) 1.3 − 1.2   n) 1.5 + 0.9   o) 2.1 − 0.7   **BONUS ▶**
                                                              2001.4 − 0.9

3. Estimate by rounding to the nearest tenth. Then add or subtract.

   a)   0.42 $\longrightarrow$ | 0.4 | b)   0.28 $\longrightarrow$ | |
         + 5.23 $\longrightarrow$ + | 5.2 | + 0.14 $\longrightarrow$ + | |
         _____   _____
              5.6

   c)   2.62 $\longrightarrow$ | | d)   4.87 $\longrightarrow$ | |
         − 0.19 $\longrightarrow$ − | | − 4.57 $\longrightarrow$ − | |
         _____   _____

   e) 0.73 + 2.17 $\approx$ _0.7 + 2.2 = 2.9_____   f) 0.89 − 0.46 $\approx$ _____

   g) 0.63 + 0.26 $\approx$ _____   h) 3.82 − 2.47 $\approx$ _____

   i) 0.48 + 2.27 $\approx$ _____   j) 126.42 − 126.37 $\approx$ _____

4. The decimal tenths that could be rounded to 7 are from 6.5 to 7.4. Which decimal tenths could be rounded to 17? Explain how you know.

For Questions 5 to 7, estimate the answer before calculating.

5. Mary wants to buy a backpack for $24.99, a tennis racket for $36.50, and a hockey shirt for $19.99. How much will the three items cost altogether?

6. The average temperature in Saint John's, NL, in April is 1.9°C. The average temperature in Saint John's, NL, in August is 15.5°C. What is the difference between the two average temperatures?

7. The school is 1.7 km from the library and 2.3 km from the house. The library is 0.7 km from the house.

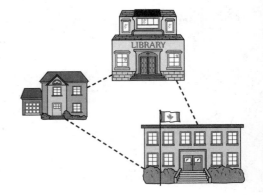

   a) Find the distance from the house to the school to the library and back to the house.

   b) How much farther is the school from the library than the library is from the house?

8. At a school track meet, the student whose long jump was 2.37 m won first prize. Second prize went to the student who jumped 2.19 m.

   a) Was the difference between the jumps more or less than 10 cm?

   b) Round both jumps to the nearest tenth. What is the difference between the rounded amounts?

   c) Make up two jumps that would round to the same number when rounded to the tenths.

NS5-60 Multiplying Decimals by Powers of 10

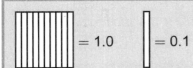 = 1.0   = 0.1

If a hundreds block represents 1 whole,
then a tens block represents 1 tenth (or 0.1), and

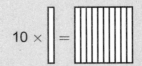

10 tenths make 1 whole:
$10 \times 0.1 = 1.0$

1. Multiply the number of tens blocks by 10. Then show how many hundreds blocks there are to complete the multiplication statement.

a) $10 \times$ [blocks] $=$ [blocks]

$10 \times 0.2 = \underline{\quad 2 \quad}$

b) $10 \times$ [blocks] $=$

$10 \times 0.3 = \underline{\qquad}$

c) $10 \times$ [blocks] $=$

$10 \times 0.5 = \underline{\qquad}$

2. Multiply by 10 by shifting the decimal point one place to the right.

a) $10 \times 0.5 = \underline{\quad 5 \quad}$

b) $10 \times 2.6 = \underline{\qquad}$

c) $10 \times 1.4 = \underline{\qquad}$

d) $10 \times 2.4 = \underline{\qquad}$

e) $3.5 \times 10 = \underline{\qquad}$

f) $14.5 \times 10 = \underline{\qquad}$

g) $10 \times 2.06 = \underline{\quad 20.6 \quad}$

h) $10 \times 12.75 = \underline{\qquad}$

i) $10 \times 97.6 = \underline{\qquad}$

To convert from metres to centimetres, you multiply by 100. There are 100 cm in 1 m.

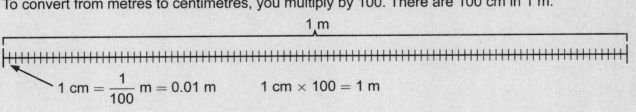

1 m

$1 \text{ cm} = \dfrac{1}{100} \text{ m} = 0.01 \text{ m}$ $1 \text{ cm} \times 100 = 1 \text{ m}$

3. Convert the measurement in metres to centimetres.

a) $0.4 \text{ m} = \underline{\qquad} \text{ cm}$

b) $0.8 \text{ m} = \underline{\qquad} \text{ cm}$

c) $3.4 \text{ m} = \underline{\qquad} \text{ cm}$

4. 10×5 can be written as a sum: $5 + 5 + 5 + 5 + 5 + 5 + 5 + 5 + 5 + 5$.
Write 10×0.5 as a sum and skip count by 0.5 to find the answer.

5. A dime is a tenth of a dollar ($10¢ = \$0.10$). Draw a picture or use play money to show that $10 \times \$0.10 = \$1.00$.

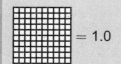 = 1.0

If a hundreds block represents 1 whole, then

 = 0.01

a ones block represents 1 hundredth (or 0.01), and

$100 \times \square = $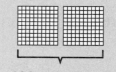

100 hundredths make 1 whole: $100 \times 0.01 = 1.00$.

6. Write a multiplication statement for the picture.

a)

$100 \times \square = $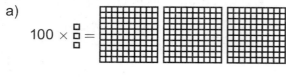

___100 × 0.03___ = _____

b)

$100 \times \square = $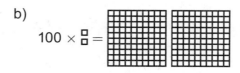

_____ = _____

The picture shows why the decimal point shifts two places to the right when multiplying by 100:

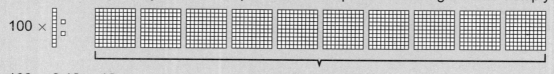

$100 \times 0.12 = 12$ $100 \times 0.1 = 10$ $100 \times 0.02 = 2$

7. Multiply by 100. Do your rough work in the grid.

a) 100×0.8 = ___80___

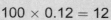

b) 100×3.5 = _____

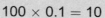

c) 7.2×100 = _____

d) 6.0×100 = _____

e) 100×0.34 = _____

f) 100×0.07 = _____

We can use zero as a placeholder when multiplying decimals. Example: 2.35×1000:

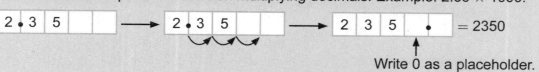

$= 2350$

Write 0 as a placeholder.

BONUS ▶ Multiply by 1000 by shifting the decimal point three places to the right.

a) $1000 \times 0.93 = $ _____

b) $6.32 \times 1000 = $ _____

c) $1000 \times 0.72 = $ _____

8. a) Fill in the table.

Metres	1	2		4		6
Centimetres	*100*		*300*		*500*	

b) To convert a measurement from metres to centimetres, you multiply by _____.

c) Write "more" or "fewer" in the blank: To change a measurement from a larger unit

to a smaller unit, you need _____ of the smaller unit.

d) Write "m" or "cm" in the blanks: In the measurement 6.04 m, the 6 stands for

_____ and the 4 stands for _____.

e) Write "as large as" or "as small as" in the blanks: Metres are 100 times _____

centimetres, and centimetres are 100 times _____ metres.

> **REMINDER ▶** To multiply a decimal by 100, shift the decimal point two places to the right.

9. Convert the measurement from metres to centimetres by multiplying by 100.

a) 5.0 m × 100 = ___*500*___ cm

b) 0.2 m × 100 = _____ cm

c) 0.83 m × 100 = _____ cm

d) 4.9 m × 100 = _____ cm

> **REMINDER ▶** There are 1000 m in 1 km. To convert from kilometres to metres, multiply by 1000.

10. Convert the measurement from kilometres to metres by multiplying by 1000.

a) 8.0 km × 1000 = ___*8000*___ m

b) 2.4 km × 1000 = _____ m

c) 0.16 km × 1000 = _____ m

d) 0.04 km × 1000 = _____ m

11. Convert the measurement.

a) 0.9 km × ___*1000*___ = _____ m

b) 3.7 m × _____ = _____ cm

c) 1.04 m × _____ = _____ cm

d) 9.02 km × _____ = _____ m

12. Kim thinks that 0.15 km plus 48 m equals 48.15 m.

a) Is her answer correct? _____

b) If her answer is not correct, explain her mistake and add the lengths correctly.

NS5-61 Multiplying and Dividing Decimals by Powers of 10

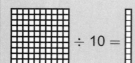 ÷ 10 =

Divide 1 whole into 10 equal parts; each part is 1 tenth.
1.0 ÷ 10 = 0.1

÷ 10 = □

Divide 1 tenth into 10 equal parts; each part is 1 hundredth.
0.1 ÷ 10 = 0.01

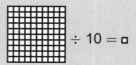 ÷ 10 = □

Divide 1 whole into 100 equal parts; each part is 1 hundredth.
1.0 ÷ 100 = 0.01

1. Complete the picture and write a division equation.

a) 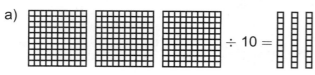 ÷ 10 =

_3.0 ÷ 10_ = _0.3_

b) 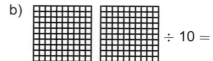 ÷ 10 =

_____ = _____

c) 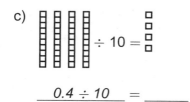 ÷ 10 =

_0.4 ÷ 10_ = _____

d) 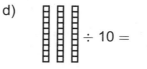 ÷ 10 =

_____ = _____

e) 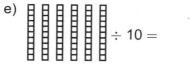 ÷ 10 =

_____ = _____

f) 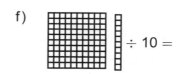 ÷ 10 =

_1.1 ÷ 10_ = _____

g) 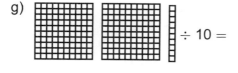 ÷ 10 =

_____ = _____

h) 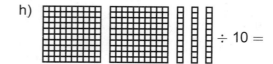 ÷ 10 =

_____ = _____

REMINDER ▶ Division can be used to "undo" a multiplication.   4 —×2→ 8 and 8 —÷2→ 4

2. How do you undo multiplying by 100 or 1000?

   a) To multiply by 100, I move the decimal point _____ places to the _____ ,

   so to divide by 100, I move the decimal point _____ places to the _____ .

   b) To multiply by 1000, I move the decimal point _____ places to the _____ ,

   so to divide by 1000, I move the decimal point _____ places to the _____ .

3. Shift the decimal point one or two places to the left. Draw an arrow to show a shift.

a) 0.4 ÷ 10 = _.04 or 0.04_

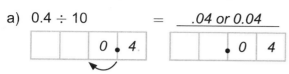

b) 0.7 ÷ 10 = _____

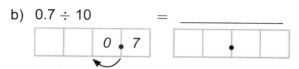

c) 0.6 ÷ 10 = _____

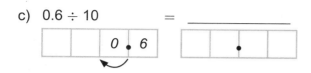

d) 3.1 ÷ 10 = _0.31_

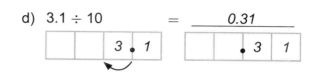

e) 15.0 ÷ 10 = _____

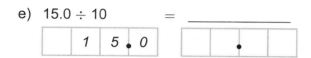

f) 81.4 ÷ 10 = _____

g) 25.4 ÷ 10 = _____

h) 23.0 ÷ 10 = _____

i) 0.5 ÷ 100 = _0.005_

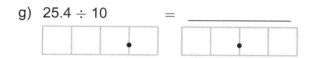

j) 7.0 ÷ 100 = _____

k) 9.1 ÷ 100 = _____

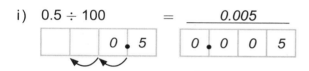

l) 91.0 ÷ 100 = _____

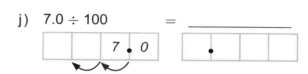

4. a) To multiply by 10, I move the decimal point __1__ place to the __right__.

b) To multiply by 1000, I move the decimal point _____ places to the _____.

c) To multiply by 10 000, I move the decimal point _____ places to the _____.

d) To divide by 100, I move the decimal point _____ places to the _____.

e) To divide by 10, I move the decimal point _____ place to the _____.

f) To multiply by 100, I move the decimal point _____ places to the _____.

g) To _____ by 10, I move the decimal point _____ place to the left.

h) To _____ by 100, I move the decimal point _____ places to the right.

i) To _____ by 10, I move the decimal point _____ place to the right.

j) To _____ by 100, I move the decimal point _____ places to the left.

k) To _____ by 1000, I move the decimal point _____ places to the right.

Number Sense 5-61

NS5-62 Decimals in Context

1. Draw a picture to show 1 tenth of the whole. For parts b) and c), draw only the outline of the shape.

   a)

   1 whole   1 tenth

   b)

   1 whole   1 tenth

   c)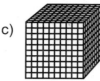

   1 whole   1 tenth

2. Add. You will have to regroup.

   a)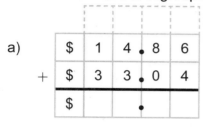

   b)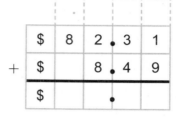

   c)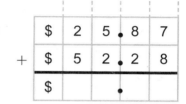

3. Subtract.

   a)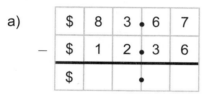

   b)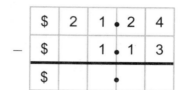

   c)

4. Subtract. You will have to regroup.

   a) $65.47 − $12.38

   b) $11.24 − $2.17

   c) $58.25 − $47.26

   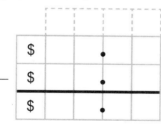   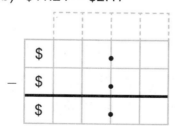

5. Alex says that it would take him longer to ride 2.50 km on his bike than it would to ride 2.5 km because 2.50 is a longer distance than 2.5. Do you agree with Alex's reasoning? Explain why or why not.

6. Write the amount in dollar notation.

   a) 808¢ = $_____

   b) 6¢ = $_____

   c) 92¢ = $_____

7. Marko has $10.25. Sandy has twice as much as Marko. How much do Marko and Sandy have altogether? Explain your thinking.

8. Nina spent $4.99 on a pencil case, $7.20 on a book, and $35.15 on a calculator. How much money did she spend altogether?

9. Jayden wants to buy a skateboard that costs $53.25. He earns $10 when he cuts someone's lawn and $15/hour for babysitting. If he babysits for 4 hours, he will earn $4 \times \$15 = \$60$ and will have enough money to buy the skateboard.

   a) How many lawns would he have to cut to be able to buy the skateboard without any babysitting?

   b) Determine one combination of babysitting and cutting lawns that Jayden could do to earn enough money to buy the skateboard. Hint: There are several possible combinations.

10. Round to the nearest whole number.

   a) 3.4 [ ]   b) 5.5 [ ]   c) 100.1 [ ]

11. Round to the nearest tenth.

   a) 19.50 [ ]   b) 7.06 [ ]   c) 0.06 [ ]

12. Estimate by rounding both numbers to the nearest tenth. Then use grid paper to add or subtract.

   a) $1.64 + 18.75$ b) $23.07 - 17.09$ c) $104.43 + 0.09$ **BONUS** ▶ $99.96 - 49.87$

13. Rick wants to buy 2 children's tickets and 1 adult ticket for a movie. Children's tickets cost $6.25 each, and adult tickets cost $13.25 each. He has $25.00. Does he have enough money?

   a) Estimate by rounding to the nearest whole number. Write "yes" or "no" in the blank.

   b) Calculate. Write "yes" or "no" in the blank.

   c) If you rounded to the nearest tenth instead of the nearest whole number in part a), would your answer have changed? Explain.

G5-12 Columns and Rows

1. Join the dots in the given column, row, or both.

   a) Column 2

   b) Row 3

   c) Row 1

   d) Column 1

   e) Column 2, Row 1

   f) Column 2, Row 3

   g) Column 3, Row 1

   h) Column 1, Row 2

2. Circle the dot in the given position.

   a) Column 2, Row 1

   b) Column 3, Row 2

   c) Column 3, Row 1

   d) Column 2, Row 2

3. Circle the dot where the two lines meet. Then identify that dot's column and row.

   a)

   Column _____

   Row _____

   b)

   Column _____

   Row _____

   c)

   Column _____

   Row _____

   d)

   Column _____

   Row _____

4. Identify the column and the row for the circled dot.

   a)

   Column _____

   Row _____

   b)

   Column _____

   Row _____

   c)

   Column _____

   Row _____

   d)

   Column _____

   Row _____

You can write the column and the row for a point in brackets.
Always write the column first.

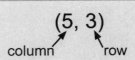

(5, 3)
column ↗   ↖ row

5. Circle the dot in the given position.

a) (2, 1)

```
3 • • •
2 • • •
1 • • •
  1 2 3
```

b) (3, 3)

```
3 • • •
2 • • •
1 • • •
  1 2 3
```

c) (1, 2)

```
3 • • •
2 • • •
1 • • •
  1 2 3
```

d) (2, 3)

```
3 • • •
2 • • •
1 • • •
  1 2 3
```

e) (3, 1)

```
3 • • •
2 • • •
1 • • •
  1 2 3
```

f) (3, 2)

```
3 • • •
2 • • •
1 • • •
  1 2 3
```

g) (1, 3)

```
3 • • •
2 • • •
1 • • •
  1 2 3
```

h) (2, 2)

```
3 • • •
2 • • •
1 • • •
  1 2 3
```

You can use letters instead of numbers to label columns and rows.

6. Circle the given point.

a) (A, 3)

```
3 • • •
2 • • •
1 • • •
  A B C
```

b) (Y, B)

```
C • • •
B • • •
A • • •
  X Y Z
```

c) (0, 2)

```
3 • • •
2 • • •
1 • • •
  0 1 2
```

d) (0, 0)

```
2 • • •
1 • • •
0 • • •
  0 1 2
```

e) (A, C)

```
D • • • •
C • • • •
B • • • •
A • • • •
  A B C D
```

f) (2, X)

```
Z • • • •
Y • • • •
X • • • •
W • • • •
  1 2 3 4
```

g) (4, 1)

```
4 • • • •
3 • • • •
2 • • • •
1 • • • •
  1 2 3 4
```

h) (3, 4)

```
4 • • • •
3 • • • •
2 • • • •
1 • • • •
  1 2 3 4
```

7. Write the position of the circled dot. Remember: the column is always given first.

a)

```
3 • ⊙ •
2 • • •
1 • • •
  1 2 3
```

(_____ , _____)

b)

```
3 • • •
2 • • ⊙
1 • • •
  1 2 3
```

(_____ , _____)

c)

```
3 • • •
2 ⊙ • •
1 • • •
  1 2 3
```

(_____ , _____)

d)

```
3 • • •
2 • • •
1 • • ⊙
  1 2 3
```

(_____ , _____)

G5-13 Coordinate Grids

An **ordered pair** is a pair of numbers in brackets that give the position of a point on a coordinate grid. The numbers are called the **coordinates** of the point.

A (3, 1)
x-coordinate   y-coordinate

B (1, 3)
x-coordinate   y-coordinate

The *x*-coordinate is always written first.

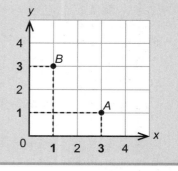

1. a) Plot and label the points on the coordinate grid.
        Cross out the coordinates as you go.

~~A (1, 4)~~   B (1, 6)   C (2, 5)

D (3, 6)   E (4, 5)   F (5, 6)

G (6, 5)   H (7, 6)   I (7, 4)

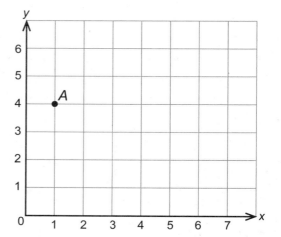

   b) Join the points in alphabetical order. Then join *A* to *I*.

   c) What does the picture you made look like?

   _____

We use number lines to mark the grid lines.
The number lines are called **axes**.
One number line is called an **axis**.
The axes meet at the point (0, 0), called the **origin**.

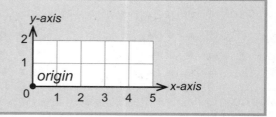

2. a) Fill in the coordinates for the given points.

A (_1_ , _3_)   B (___, ___)   C (___, ___)

D (___, ___)   E (___, ___)   F (___, ___)

G (___, ___)   H (___, ___)   I (___, ___)

J (___, ___)   K (___, ___)   L (___, ___)

   b) Which points are on the *x*-axis? _____

   c) Which points are on the *y*-axis? _____

   d) Which point is on both axes? _____

   e) Which point is the origin? _____

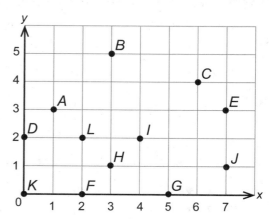

3. a) Plot and label the points on the coordinate grid.
Cross out the coordinates as you plot them.

A (0, 4)   B (0, 5)   C (5, 5)

D (5, 4)   E (3, 4)   F (3, 0)

G (2, 0)   H (2, 4)

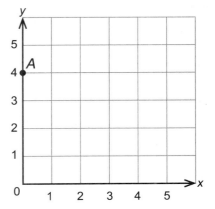

b) Join the points in alphabetical order. Then join A to H.

c) What letter have you drawn? _____

4. a) Find the coordinates of the points.

A (__1__ , __9__)   B (_____ , _____)

C (_____ , _____)   D (_____ , _____)

E (_____ , _____)   F (_____ , _____)

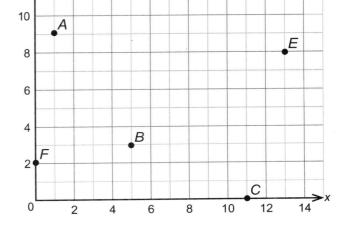

b) Plot and label the points.

G (4, 6)   H (7, 10)   I (10, 7)

J (5, 9)   K (3, 0)   L (0, 7)

M (13, 11)   N (7, 5)   O (0, 0)

5. a) Mark the points on the number line.

A 38   B 14   C 27   D 49

b) Label the points marked on the coordinate grid.
Use a ruler to line up the points with the axes.

A (5, 15)   B (50, 20)

C (48, 3)   D (0, 13)

E (15, 10)   F (30, 26)

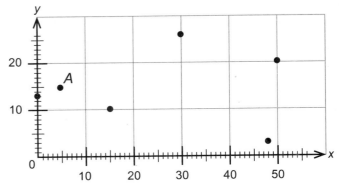

BONUS ▶ Use a ruler to mark the points on the
coordinate grid.

G (5, 0)   H (25, 10)

I (40, 15)   J (35, 5)

6. a) Draw a coordinate grid on 1 cm grid paper. Skip count by 5s to label the axes.

b) Plot the points in each group and join them to create a polygon. Identify the polygons.

i) Q (10, 0), R (5, 10), S (20, 15)   ii) T (5, 15), U (5, 25), V (20, 25), W (20, 15)

G5-14 Congruence and Symmetry

Karen places shapes one on top of the other. She tries to make the shapes match.

If they match exactly, the shapes are **congruent**.

Congruent shapes have the same size and shape.

Congruent shapes 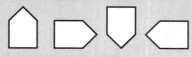 Not congruent shapes

1. Are the shapes congruent? Write "yes" or "no."

a) 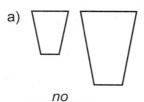   b) 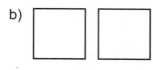   c) 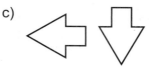   d)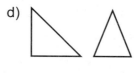

____no____   _____   _____   _____

e) 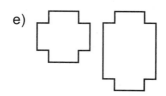   f) 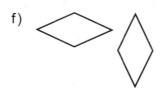   g) 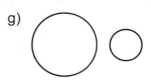   h)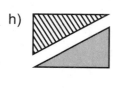

_____   _____   _____   _____

2. Circle the two congruent shapes.

a)   b)

c)   d)

3. Draw a shape congruent to the shaded shape. Then draw another polygon of the given type that is not congruent to the shaded shape.

a) a square

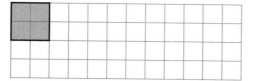

b) a triangle

4. Choose two shapes from Question 3 part a) that are not congruent. Explain why they are not congruent.

5. Jax draws a line to break the shape into two parts. Are the parts of the shape congruent?

a)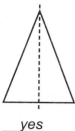

_____yes_____

b)

_____

c)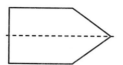

_____

d)

_____

> When you can fold a shape in half so that the parts match exactly, the fold is called a **line of symmetry**.
>
> Parts match exactly.   Parts do not match.
>
>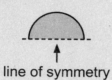
>
> line of symmetry   not a line of symmetry

6. Is the dashed line a line of symmetry?

a)

_____yes_____

b)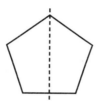

_____

c)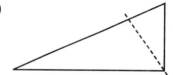

_____

d)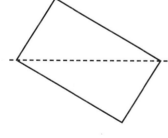

_____

e)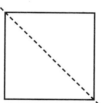

_____

f)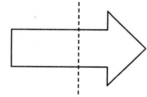

_____

7. Draw a line of symmetry. Use a ruler.

a)

b)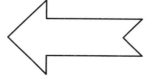

c)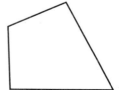

8. Draw all the lines of symmetry for the shape.

a)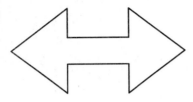

b)

c)

d)

e)

f)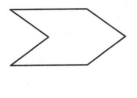

9. The dashed line is the line of symmetry. Draw the missing part of the picture. Use a ruler.

a)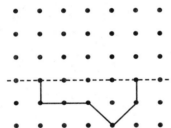

b)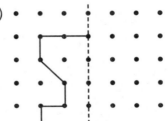

c)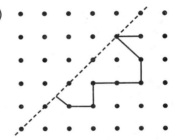

BONUS ▶ Draw the missing parts. Then draw another line of symmetry.

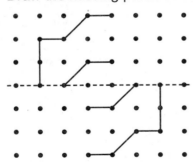

10. Draw a picture that has a line of symmetry in the given direction.

    a) horizontal   b) vertical   c) diagonal

11. Draw a figure with more than one line of symmetry. How many lines of symmetry does it have? What are the lines of symmetry?

BONUS ▶ Draw a shape that has more than 6 lines of symmetry.

G5-15 Translations

Josh slides a dot from one position to another. To move the dot from position 1 to position 2, Josh slides the dot 4 units right. In mathematics, slides are called **translations**.

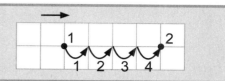

1. How many units **right** did the dot slide from position 1 to position 2?

a)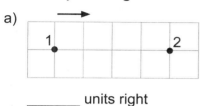

_____ units right

b)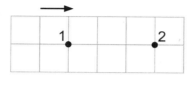

_____

c)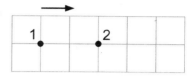

_____

2. How many units **left** did the dot slide from position 1 to position 2?

a)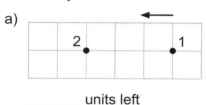

_____ units left

b)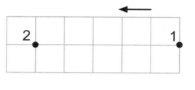

_____

c)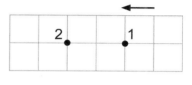

_____

3. Follow the instructions to translate the dot to a new position.

a) 3 units right

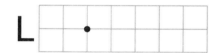

b) 2 units left

c) 6 units right

4. Describe the translation of the dot from position 1 to position 2.

a)

_____ units right

_____ units down

b)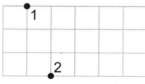

_____ unit right

_____ units down

c)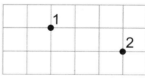

_____ units right

_____ unit down

5. Translate the dot.

a) 5 units right, 3 units down

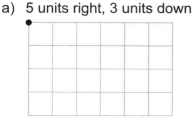

b) 5 units left, 1 unit up

c) 4 units left, 3 units down

6. Copy the shaded shape onto the second grid. (Make sure your shape is in the same position relative to the dot.)

a)    b) 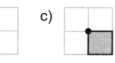   c)   d)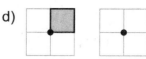

e)   f)   g)    h)

7. Copy the shape onto the second grid.

a) 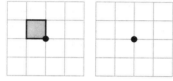   b) 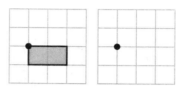   c)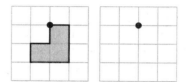

> When you slide a shape, the shape in the new position is called the **image**.

8. Slide the shape 4 units right. Make sure the dot is at the right place in the image.

a)   b)    c)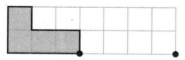

9. Slide the shape 3 units in the direction shown. First slide the dot, then copy the shape.

a) 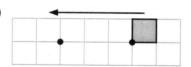   b) 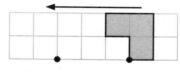   c)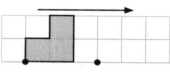

d)    e) 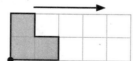   f)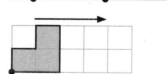

10. Slide the dot three units down, then copy the shape.

a) 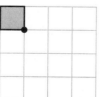   b)   c) 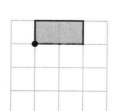   d)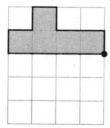

Geometry 5-15

To translate a shape 4 units right and 1 unit down:

Step 1: Draw a dot on a corner of the shape.

Step 2: Slide the dot 4 units right and 1 unit down.

Step 3: Draw the image of the shape.

You can draw a **translation arrow** to show the direction of the slide.

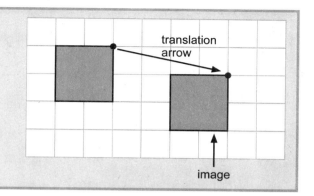

11. Slide the shape 4 units right. Draw a translation arrow.

a)

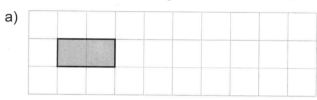

b)

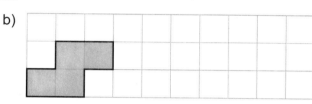

c)

d)

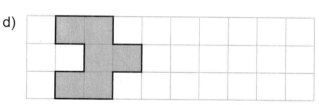

12. Slide the shape 5 units right and 2 units down. Draw a translation arrow.

a)

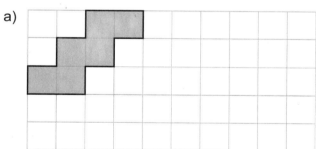

b)

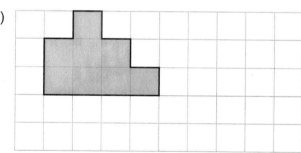

13. Can the pair of shapes be created by a translation? If so, describe the translation. If not, explain why not.

a)

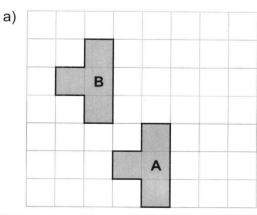

b)

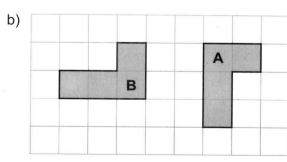

G5-16 Maps

1. This is a star map of the Big Dipper, which is part of the Great Bear constellation.

   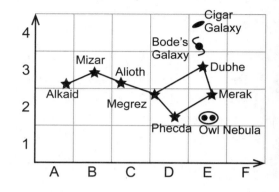

   a) Which star is in square E3? _____

   b) Which star is in square C3? _____

   c) The star "Alkaid" is in square _____.

   d) The Owl Nebula is in square _____.

      What else is in that square? _____

   e) How many squares up from the Owl Nebula

      is Bode's Galaxy? _____

   f) Which star is 2 squares left and 1 square up from Phecda? _____

   BONUS ▶ The Pinwheel Galaxy is located two squares left and one square up from Alioth.

   Mark the galaxy on the map. What square is it in? _____

2. This map shows part of Feral Cat Island, where pirates have buried gold, silver, and weapons. Fill in the directions.

   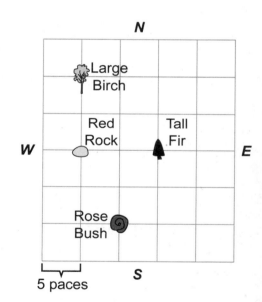

   a) From the Tall Fir, walk ___10___ paces (steps) _____west_____ to the Red Rock.

   b) From the Red Rock, walk _____ paces north to the Large Birch.

   c) From the Red Rock, walk _____ paces _____

      and _____ paces east to the Rose Bush.

   d) From the Rose Bush, walk _____ paces _____

      and _____ paces _____ to the Tall Fir.

   e) From the Tall Fir, walk _____ and

      _____ to the Large Birch.

3. Mark on the map in Question 2 the point where some treasure is buried.

   a) Gold (G): From the Tall Fir, walk 5 paces east and 10 paces north.

      Weapons (W): From the Rose Bush, walk 10 paces west and 5 paces south.

      Silver (S): From the Large Birch, walk 10 paces south and 5 paces east.

   b) What two landmarks is the silver buried between? _____

   c) Write directions for walking from Gold to Silver.

   _____

   _____

4. This map shows all of Feral Cat Island. Each square on the map has sides 2 km long.

a) Round Lake is located at point (4, 8). What is located at each point?

(6, 4) _____

(6, 10) _____

(10, 7) _____

(12, 10) _____

Feral Cat Island

b) Give the coordinates for each landmark.

Old Lighthouse _____

Lookout Hill _____

The Fort _____

c) Name the landmark located at each point described.

2 km east of the Fort _____

4 km south of Round Lake _____

BONUS ▶ 2 km north and 3 km west of the Treasure _____

d) Fill in the blanks.

From Round Lake, the Old Lighthouse is ___*10*___ km _____*east*_____.

From the Fort, walk _____ km _____ to the Treasure.

From the Treasure, the Bear Cave is _____ km _____.

To walk from the Bear Cave to Lookout Hill, walk _____ km _____ and

_____ km south.

From Fang Cliff, walk _____ km _____ and _____ km

_____ to Clear Spring.

From the Fort, walk _____ to the Bear Cave.

From Lookout Hill to the Treasure, travel _____.

From the Old Lighthouse to the Bear Cave, travel _____.

e) Write your own question that asks for directions and uses the map. Ask your partner to answer it.

_____

_____

_____

G5-17 Reflections

1. Draw the line of symmetry.

a)
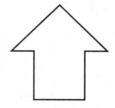

b)

c)

2. The dashed line is the mirror line. Draw the mirror image.

a)
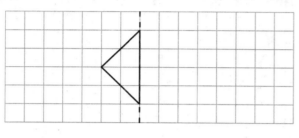

b)
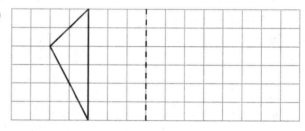

c)
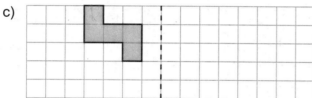

d)
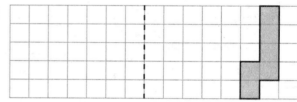

3. a) The dashed line is the reflecting line. Draw the mirror image.

i)
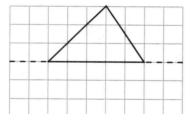

ii)
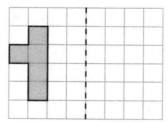

iii)
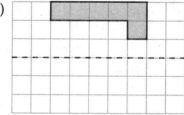

b) For each shape in part a), choose one vertex of the original shape. Draw a dot on that vertex and a dot on the image of that point. Fill in the table.

	Distance Between Original Vertex and Reflecting Line	Distance Between Image Vertex and Reflecting Line
i)		
ii)		
iii)		

c) What do you notice about your answers in part b)?

_____

_____

4. Draw the reflections of the shape and points in the line.

a)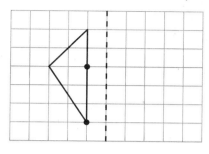

b)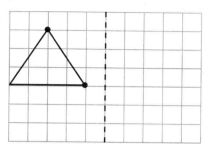

c)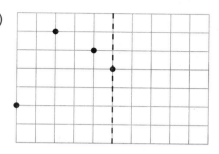

d)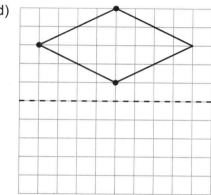

e)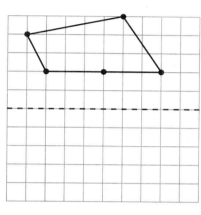

f)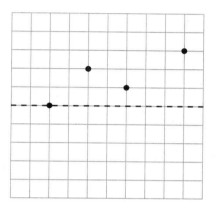

5. Draw the reflection of the shape by first finding the reflections of its vertices.

a)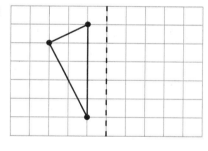

b)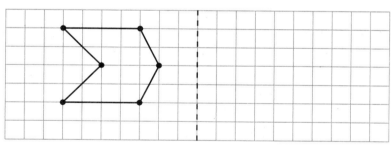

c)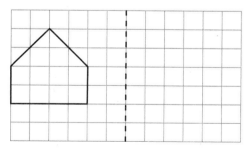

d)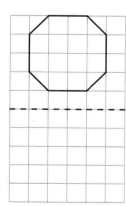

BONUS ▶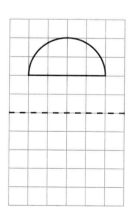

6. a) Extend the patterns by reflecting the shapes in vertical lines.

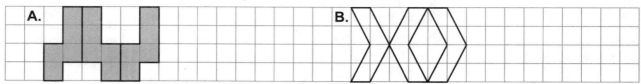

b) Draw the 14th shape in pattern A.

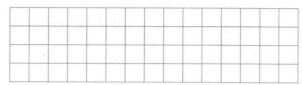

c) Draw the 67th shape in pattern A.

d) Draw the 17th shape in pattern B.

e) Draw the 80th shape in pattern B.

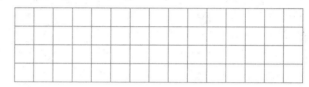

7. a) Colour the squares in the first 3 by 3 tile using at least two colours. Make sure your coloured tile does not have a line of symmetry. Create a pattern by reflecting your tile vertically and horizontally to cover the whole grid.

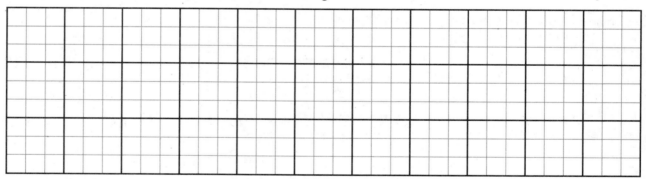

b) What would the 8th tile in the fourth column look like?

c) What would the 9th tile in the fifth column look like?

G5-18 Reflections and Translations

1. Find the vertical line of reflection.

a) 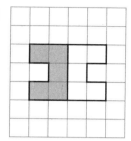 b) 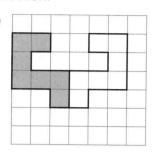 c) 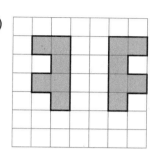 d)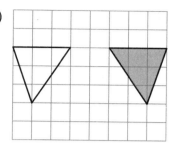

2. Find the horizontal line of reflection.

a) 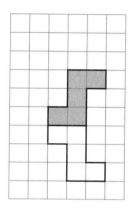 b) 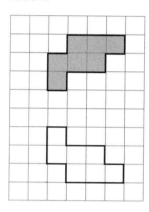 c) 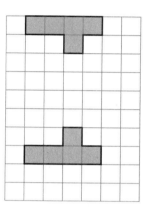 BONUS ▶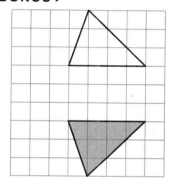

3. Draw the line of reflection or a translation arrow.

a) 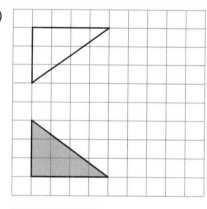 b) 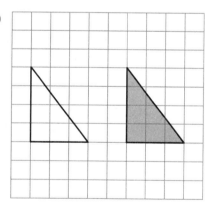 c)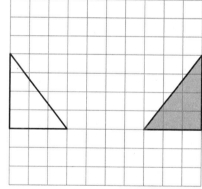

d) 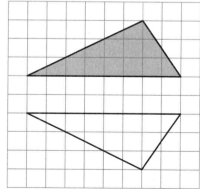 e) 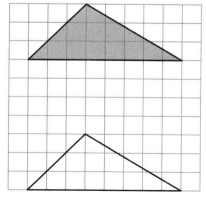 BONUS ▶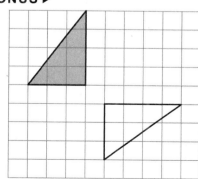

4. Circle the pairs that can be created by a reflection. Put a check mark beside pairs that can be created by a translation.

a)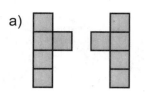

b)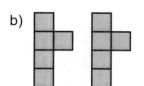

c)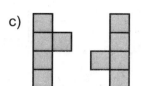

d)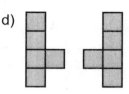

e)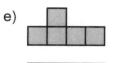

f)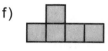

g)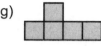

h)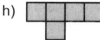

i)

j)

BONUS ▶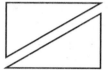

5. Use the shapes in Question 4 to complete the question.

a) Use a ruler to draw the lines of reflection in the circled pairs of shapes.

b) Draw a translation arrow for the pairs of shapes with check marks.

c) Which pair of shapes can be created by a reflection or a translation? _____

6. Use the word "same" or "opposite" to fill in the blank.

a) When a shape is reflected, the image faces the _____ direction.

b) When a shape is translated, the image faces the _____ direction.

7. Tessa says that if you reflect or translate any shape, the image and the original shape are always congruent. Do you agree with Tessa? Explain.

_____

_____

8. The pattern is made by translations. Continue the pattern. Then draw translation arrows and circle the core of the pattern.

a)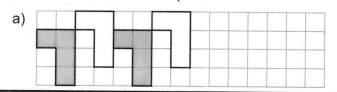

b)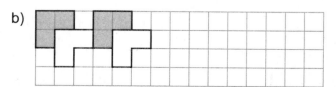

Geometry 5-18

9. David made a pattern by alternating between reflecting and translating a shape.

   a) Continue the pattern.

   b) Draw the core of the pattern.

   c) Draw the 19th shape in the pattern.

   d) Draw the 26th shape in the pattern.

10. a) Use reflections and translations to draw your own pattern of shapes.

   b) Draw the core of the pattern you drew in part a).

   c) Use translations only to draw your own pattern of shapes.

   d) Draw the core of the pattern you drew in part c).

G5-19 Rotations

1. Write the amount shaded as a whole (1) or a fraction.

a) $\frac{1}{4}$

b)

c)

d)

e)

f)

g)

h)

The direction in which a clock hand moves is called **clockwise (CW)**.

The opposite direction is called **counter-clockwise (CCW)**.

2. Shade the part of the circle the clock hand has moved across. Write the fraction of a turn.

a)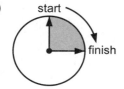

$\boxed{\frac{1}{4}}$ turn CW

b)

☐ turn CW

c)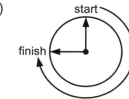

☐ turn CW

d)

☐ turn CW

e)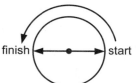

☐ turn CCW

f)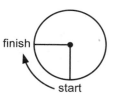

☐ turn CW

g)

☐ turn CCW

h)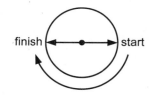

☐ turn CW

i)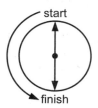

☐ _____

j)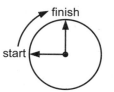

☐ _____

k)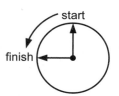

☐ _____

BONUS ▶

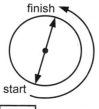

☐ _____

3. Write the fraction of a turn the arrow has moved from start to finish.

a)

$\boxed{\dfrac{1}{4}}$ turn CW

b)

$\Box$ turn CW

c)

$\Box$ _____

d)

$\Box$ _____

e)

$\Box$ turn CCW

f)

$\Box$ turn CCW

g)

$\Box$ _____

h)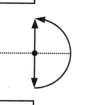

$\Box$ _____

Marla wants to **rotate** this arrow $\dfrac{1}{4}$ of a turn clockwise.

First she draws a curved arrow to show the size of the **rotation.**

Then she draws the final position of the arrow.

 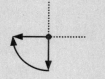

---

4. Show where the arrow would be after the given rotation. Use Marla's method.

a)

$\dfrac{1}{4}$ turn clockwise

b)

$\dfrac{1}{2}$ turn clockwise

c)

$\dfrac{3}{4}$ turn clockwise

d)

1 whole turn clockwise

e)

$\dfrac{1}{2}$ turn counter-clockwise

f)

1 whole turn counter-clockwise

g)

$\dfrac{1}{4}$ turn counter-clockwise

h)

$\dfrac{3}{4}$ turn counter-clockwise

BONUS ▶

i)

three $\dfrac{1}{4}$ turns counter-clockwise

j)

three $\dfrac{1}{2}$ turns clockwise

k)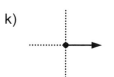

three $\dfrac{1}{4}$ turns counter-clockwise

l)

two $\dfrac{3}{4}$ turns counter-clockwise

5. Show what the figure would look like after the given rotation around point *P*. First rotate the dark line, then draw the rest of the figure.

a)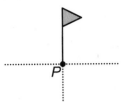

$\dfrac{1}{4}$ turn clockwise

b)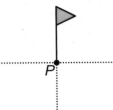

$\dfrac{1}{2}$ turn clockwise

c)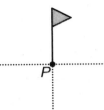

$\dfrac{3}{4}$ turn clockwise

d)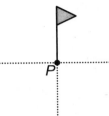

1 whole turn clockwise

e)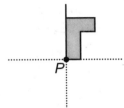

$\dfrac{1}{4}$ turn clockwise

f)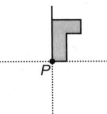

$\dfrac{1}{2}$ turn clockwise

g)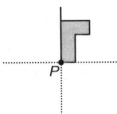

$\dfrac{3}{4}$ turn counter-clockwise

h)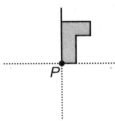

$\dfrac{1}{4}$ turn counter-clockwise

i)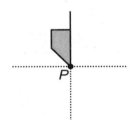

$\dfrac{1}{4}$ turn clockwise

j)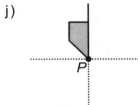

$\dfrac{3}{4}$ turn clockwise

k)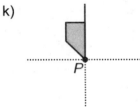

$\dfrac{1}{2}$ turn counter-clockwise

l)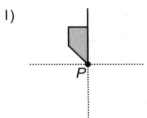

$\dfrac{1}{2}$ turn clockwise

In Question 5, point *P* is called the **centre of rotation**. It is the one point that does not move during a rotation.

6. a) Draw a 2-D shape on the grid. Label the vertices with letters. Make sure one edge is on the dark line and one vertex is on the dot.

b) Rotate your shape around the dot. Draw the image.

c) Write the fraction of the turn, the direction of the turn (clockwise or counter-clockwise), and the centre of rotation.

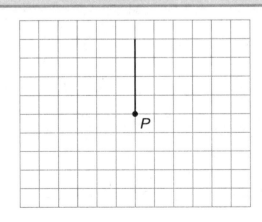

_____ around point _____.

G5-20 Translations, Reflections, and Rotations

1. Rotate the shape $\frac{1}{4}$ turn around point P in the direction shown. Draw the image.

a)   b)   c)   d)   e)

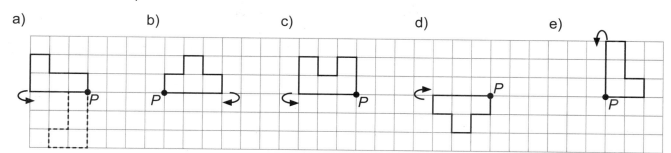

2. a) Rotate shape A $\frac{1}{2}$ turn clockwise around point P.
   Draw the image in red.

   b) Reflect shape B in the line M. Draw the image in blue.

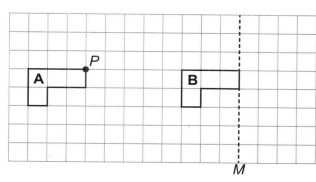

   c) Compare the red image and the blue image you drew in parts a) and b). How are they the same? How are they different? _____

   _____

   _____

3. a) Draw the image after the given translation or reflection.

   i) slide 2 units left, 1 unit down
   ii) reflect in line M
   iii) reflect in line R
   iv) slide 2 units right, 3 units down

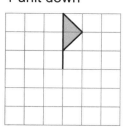 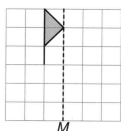 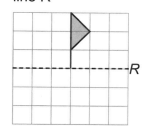 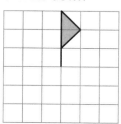

   b) Which way does the flag point now? Use N, E, S, or W.

   i) The flag points _____.
   ii) The flag points _____.
   iii) The flag points _____.
   iv) The flag points _____.

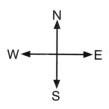

4. a) Draw the image after the rotation around point *P*.

i) $\frac{1}{4}$ turn clockwise   ii) $\frac{1}{2}$ turn counter-clockwise   iii) $\frac{3}{4}$ turn CW   iv) 1 whole turn CCW

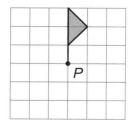 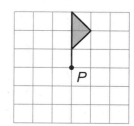 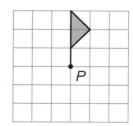 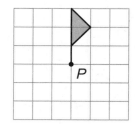

b) Which way does the flag point now? Use N, E, S, or W.

i) The flag points _____.

ii) The flag points _____.

iii) The flag points _____.

iv) The flag points _____.

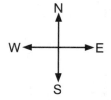

5. Describe the transformation used to move the triangle from position 1 to position 2. The sides of each square in the picture are one unit long.

a)

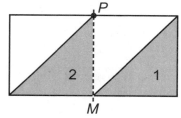

translation: one unit

left

b)

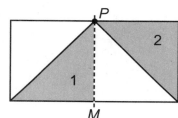

_____

_____

c)

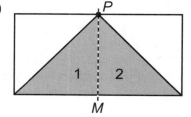

_____

_____

d)

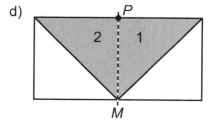

_____

_____

e)

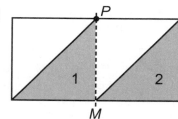

_____

_____

f)

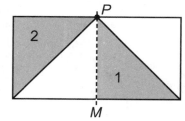

_____

_____

6. Using either a translation, reflection, or rotation, move the triangle from position 1 to a position 2 of your choice. Draw the image triangle and describe the transformation you used.

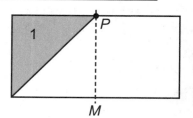

_____

7. Describe one transformation that moves the triangle from position 1 to position 2.

a)
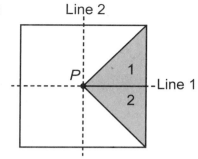

b)
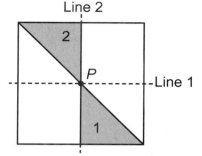

c)
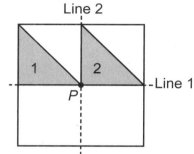

d)
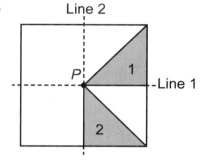

BONUS ▶ Is the statement always true, sometimes true, or never true? Explain how you know.

a) A shape and its image after a reflection face the same direction.

_____

_____

b) A shape and its image after a rotation face the same direction.

_____

_____

8. a) Use grid paper to draw a 2-D shape that has no lines of symmetry.

  i) Translate the shape. Describe the translation.

  ii) Rotate the shape. Write the fraction of the turn and the direction of the turn and then label the point of rotation.

  iii) Reflect the shape. Draw the line of reflection.

b) For each transformation in part a), compare the image to the original shape. How are they the same? How are they different?

G5-21 3-D Shapes

REMINDER ▶ 3-D shapes have **faces**, **edges**, and **vertices**.

Faces are flat. They meet at edges. Edges meet at vertices.

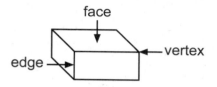 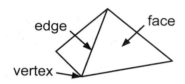

1. What is the shape of the shaded face?

a)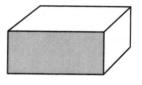

b)

c)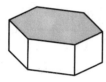

_____

d)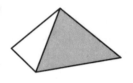

e)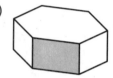

f)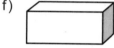

_____

2. Draw a dot on each vertex you see.

a)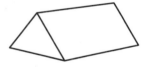

b)

c)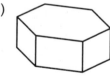

3. Trace the edges you see.

a)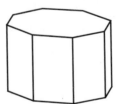

b)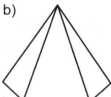

c)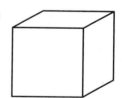

d)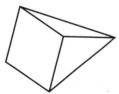

e)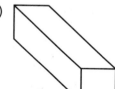

f)

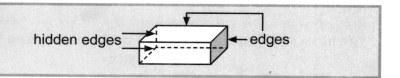

Hidden edges are shown with dashed lines.   hidden edges ← → edges

4. Draw dashed lines to show the hidden edges.

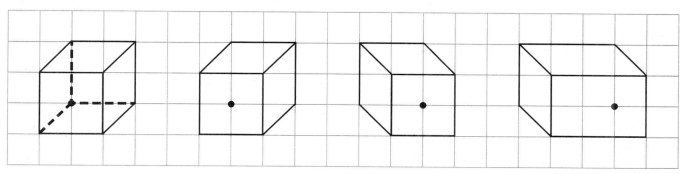

5. Trace and count the edges.

a)

_____ edges

b)

_____ edges

c)

_____ edges

d)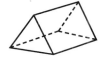

_____ edges

6. Draw a dot on each vertex. Count the vertices.

a)

_____ vertices

b)

_____ vertices

c)

_____ vertices

d)

_____ vertices

7. Imagine the shape is placed on a table. Trace the edges that would be hidden.

a)

b)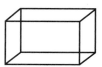

c)

d)

e)

f)

g)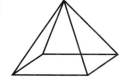

h)

In a 3-D shape, two edges that meet at a vertex are called **intersecting edges**.
Two faces that meet at an edge are called **intersecting faces**.

intersecting
edges

intersecting
faces

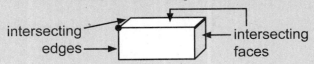

8. Do the marked edges or faces intersect? Write "yes" or "no." If they intersect,
   trace the edge or mark the vertex where they meet.

a)

___no___

b)

_____

c)

_____

d)

_____

e)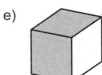

_____

f)

_____

g)

_____

h)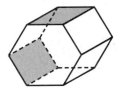

_____

The shaded faces meet at the marked vertex, not at an edge.

Faces that meet at a vertex are also called **intersecting faces**.

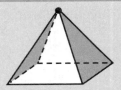

9. Do the two shaded faces intersect? Write "yes" or "no." If they intersect, trace the edge
   or mark the vertex where they meet.

a)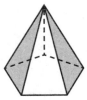

_____

b)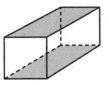

_____

c)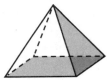

_____

d)

_____

e)

_____

f)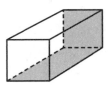

_____

g)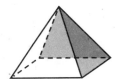

_____

h)

_____

Geometry 5-21

G5-22 Triangular and Rectangular Prisms

Prisms have two identical opposite faces called **bases**.

The bases of **triangular** prisms are triangles.

The bases of **rectangular** prisms are rectangles.

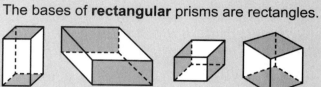

On rectangular prisms, any pair of opposite faces can be called bases.

1. Shade the bases of the prism. Then name the prism.

   a)   b)   c)   d)

   triangular

   prism   _____   _____   _____

2. Cross out the objects that are not prisms. Shade the bases of the triangular prisms.
   Circle the rectangular prisms.

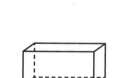 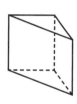 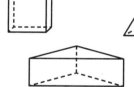  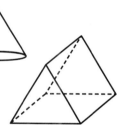

To make a skeleton of a prism:

Step 1
Make two copies of the same polygon using clay balls for vertices and toothpicks for edges. They are the bases of the prism.

Step 2
Add a toothpick to each vertex of one of the bases.

Step 3
Attach the other base on top of the toothpicks.

3. Fill in the table using skeletons of prisms.

Shape of Base	triangle	rectangle	square
Number of Vertices			
Number of Edges			

4. Connect the matching vertices with edges to finish drawing the skeleton of the prism.

a)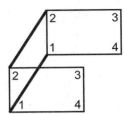

b)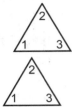

c)

5. Draw the skeleton of a triangular prism by following these steps:

Step 1: Draw the two identical triangular bases, a little bit apart and to the side.

Step 2: Connect the vertices of the bases in pairs: the bottom-left corner of one base goes to the bottom-left corner of the other, and so on.

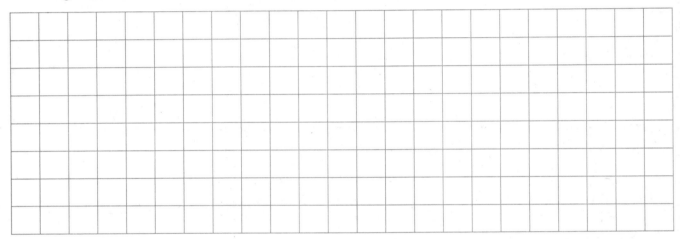

6. Fill in the table. Use actual 3-D shapes to help you.

Shape	Number of Triangular Faces	Number of Rectangular Faces
triangular prism		
rectangular prism		

7. How do you know this shape is not a triangular prism?

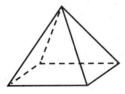

8. Sam says that in a prism, the two bases are not intersecting faces.
Do you agree with Sam? Explain.

BONUS ▶ In a triangular prism, Tasha finds two faces that do not intersect.
What are the shapes of the faces? Explain how you know.

G5-23 Prisms and Pyramids

> **REMINDER ▶** Any polygon can be the base of a prism. Examples:
>
>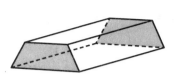
> trapezoid-based prism
>
>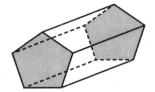
> pentagon-based prism
>
>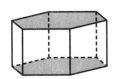
> hexagon-based prism

1. Shade a base of the prism. Then name the prism.

a)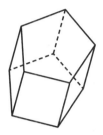

_____-based prism

b)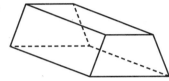

_____-based prism

c)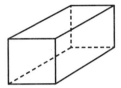

_____-based prism

d)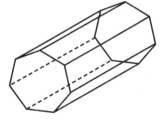

_____-based prism

e)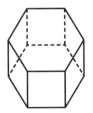

_____-based prism

f)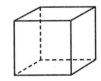

_____-based prism

> The faces in a prism that are not bases are called **side faces**.

2. Use pattern blocks to build a prism with a rhombus as its base.

   a) How many vertices does your prism have? _____

   b) How many edges does your prism have? _____

   c) How many side faces does your prism have? _____

   d) How many faces does your prism have? _____

   e) Draw all the faces.

Marko puts two prisms on a table.

In a **right prism**, the side faces are rectangles and the top base is directly above the bottom base.

In a **skew prism**, the side faces are parallelograms and the top base is not directly above the bottom base.

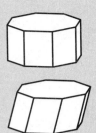

3. Shade a base of the prism. Is the prism right or skew?

a)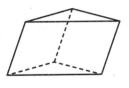

_____

b)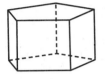

_____

c)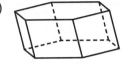

_____

4. Use actual 3-D shapes or skeletons to fill in the table.

Shape of Base of Prism	Number of ...			
	Side Faces	Faces	Vertices	Edges
rectangle				
trapezoid				
pentagon				
hexagon				

BONUS ▶ A prism has a 9-sided base.

a) How many side faces does the prism have? _____

b) How many faces does the prism have? _____

c) How many vertices does the prism have? _____

d) How many edges does the prism have? _____

e) Draw all the faces.

Pyramids have one base and a vertex opposite to the base, called the **apex**.

The bases of **triangular** pyramids are triangles.   The bases of **rectangular** pyramids are rectangles.

  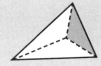

apex →

Any face of a triangular pyramid can be called a base.

5. Shade the base and draw a dot on the vertex opposite the base. Then name the pyramid.

a) 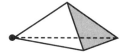   b) 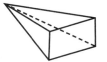   c)   d)

_triangular_____

_pyramid_____   _____   _____   _____

6. Shade the base or bases. Then name the prism or pyramid.

a)   b)   c)   d)

_____   _____   _____   _____

_____   _____   _____   _____

e) 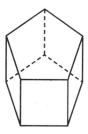   f) 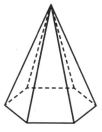   g) 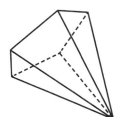   h)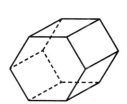

_____   _____   _____   _____

_____   _____   _____   _____

7. Draw a dot on the apex of each pyramid in Question 6.

8. **a)** Complete the table. Use actual 3-D shapes to help you.

Shape	Name of Shape	Number of ...			Picture of Faces
		Vertices	Edges	Faces	

b) Circle the bases in the last column of the table.

c) The side faces of pyramids are _____ .

9. An object has a 9-sided base and 10 vertices. Is it a prism or a pyramid? Explain.

_____

_____

_____

10. A 3-D shape has two faces that do not intersect. Can it be a pyramid? Explain.

BONUS ▶

a) An object has 10 vertices and 18 edges. Is it a pyramid or a prism? How many sides does its base have? Explain how you know.

b) An object has 16 vertices and 24 edges. Is it a pyramid or a prism? How many sides does its base have? Explain how you know.

G5-24   Parallel and Perpendicular in 3-D Shapes

Clara places 3-D shapes on a table.

Edges and faces that run straight up and down are vertical.

Edges and faces that run side to side like the table-top are horizontal.

The bases of the prism are horizontal.   The base of the pyramid is horizontal.

All of the side faces are vertical.   None of the side faces are vertical.

1. Imagine the shape is on a table. One face is shaded or one edge is darkened.
Is it vertical, horizontal, or neither?

a)

vertical

b)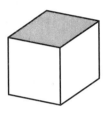

c)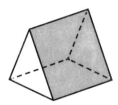

d)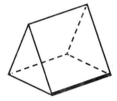

Faces that run in the same direction and are always
the same distance apart are called **parallel faces**.

To check if two faces are parallel, place one face flat on a table and
check if the other face is also horizontal.

In the shape at the right, the shaded faces are parallel.

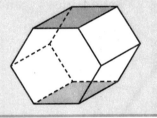

2. Are the shaded faces parallel? Write "yes" or "no." Use actual 3-D shapes if you need to.

a)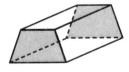

b)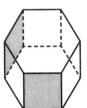

c)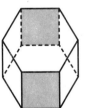

BONUS ▶

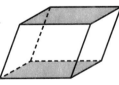

d)

e)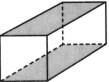

f)

BONUS ▶

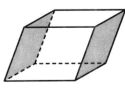

Faces that meet at a right angle are **perpendicular faces**. To check if two faces are perpendicular, place one face flat on a table and check if the other face is vertical.

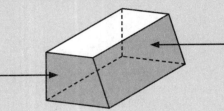

This front face is perpendicular to the bottom face.

This slanted face is not perpendicular to the bottom face.

3. Are the shaded faces perpendicular? Write "yes" or "no." Use actual 3-D shapes if you need to.

a)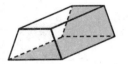

b)

c)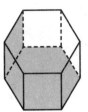

d)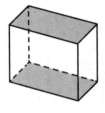

_____   _____   _____   _____

4. Are the darkened edges parallel, perpendicular, or neither?

a)

b)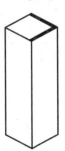

c)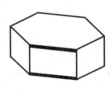

d)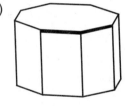

_____   _____   _____   _____

5. Are the shaded faces parallel, perpendicular, or neither?

a)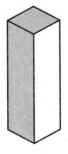

b)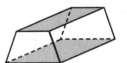

c)

d)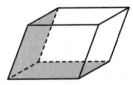

_____   _____   _____   _____

G5-25 Nets of Prisms

1. Complete the table.

| Shape | Name of Shape | Number of ... | | | Picture of Faces |
		Vertices	Edges	Faces	

A **net** of a 3-D shape is a pattern that you can fold to make the shape.

and   and   each fold into

---

2. Match the net to the 3-D object.

A.   **B.**   **C.**   **D.**   **E.**

a)   b)   c)   d)    e)

_____   _____   _____   _____   _____

G5-26 Nets of Prisms and Pyramids

1. Match the net to the 3-D object.

A.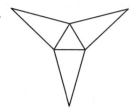

B.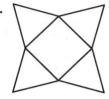

C.

a)

_____

b)

_____

c)

_____

2. Does the net make a cube? Write "yes" or "no."

a)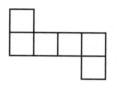

_____

b)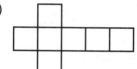

_____

c)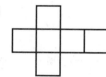

_____

d)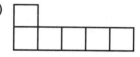

_____

e)

_____

f)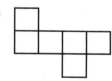

_____

3. Does the net make a square-based pyramid? Write "yes" or "no."

a)

_____

b)

_____

c)

_____

d)

_____

4. Draw the missing face for the net.

a)

b)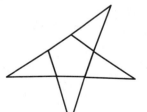

c)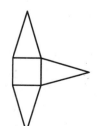

d)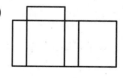

5. Create a net for the object.

a)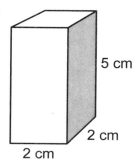

b)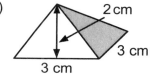

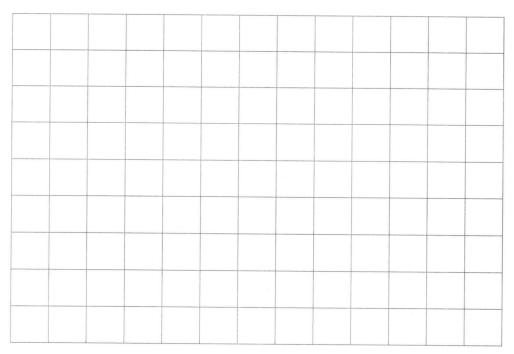

BONUS ▶ Eddy is making a model of a building out of cardboard. The building is a rectangular prism. The length and width are both 3 cm, and the height is 4 times the width.

    a) Sketch the prism.

    b) Draw a net for the model.

ME5-12 Perimeter

1. Fill in the table.

a)

m	cm
1	
2	
3	
25	

b)

cm	mm
1	
2	
3	
37	

c)

km	m
1	
2	
3	
75	

2. The table shows the lengths of some animals at the zoo.

a) Mark the lengths of **L**, **R**, **B**, and **W** on the number line.

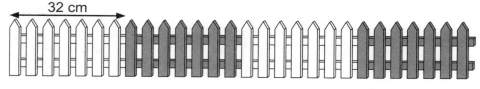

0 cm   100 cm   200 cm

Animal	Length
Lynx: **L**	150 cm
Rabbit: **R**	50 cm
Beaver: **B**	100 cm
Wolf: **W**	2 m

b) How many centimetres longer than a lynx is a wolf? _____

3. A fence is made of four parts joined end to end. Each part is 32 cm long.

32 cm

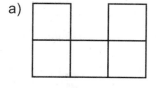

a) How long is the fence in centimetres? _____

b) Is the fence longer or shorter than a metre? _____

> The distance around the outside of a shape is called the **perimeter** of the shape.
>
> The perimeter of this figure is 5 cm because each line segment is 1 cm long.
>
>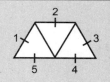

4. Each square side is 1 cm long. Find the perimeter in centimetres.

a)

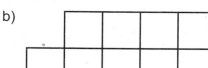

_____ cm

b)

_____ cm

c)

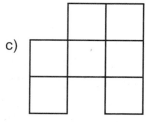

_____ cm

5. Measure the perimeter of the figure in centimetres. Use a ruler.

a)

_____

b)

_____

c)

_____

6. a) Find the perimeter of each figure (include the units).

7 m

5 m   **E**

Perimeter: _____

3 cm   2 cm

5 cm

6 cm   **U**

8 cm   4 cm

Perimeter: _____

2 km   **P**   2 km

2 km

Perimeter: _____

5 cm

R   10 cm

Perimeter: _____

b) Write the letters from the figures in order from greatest to least perimeter.
They should spell a country in South America. Hint: Watch the units!

_____ _____ _____ _____

7. Estimate the perimeter of the figure in centimetres. Then measure the actual
perimeter with a ruler.

a)

Estimated perimeter: _____

Actual perimeter: _____

b)

Estimated perimeter: _____

Actual perimeter: _____

8. a) Write the perimeter of each figure in the sequence (each square side is 1 unit).

_____   _____   _____   _____

b) How does the perimeter change each time a square is added in part a)?

_____

c) What would the perimeter of the 6th figure be? _____

9. a) Write the perimeter of each figure in the sequence (each side is 1 unit).

_____   _____   _____   _____

b) How does the perimeter change each time a hexagon is added in part a)?

_____

c) What would the perimeter of the 6th figure be? _____

10. a) Perimeter: _____

Add one square so that the perimeter of the figure increases by 2.

New perimeter: _____

b) Perimeter: _____

Add one square so that the perimeter of the figure stays the same.

New perimeter: _____

11. Draw your own figure and find its perimeter.

12. The pictures (**A** and **B**) show two ways to make a rectangle using four squares.

A.   **B.**

a) Which figure has the shorter perimeter? How do you know?

b) Are there any other ways to make a rectangle using 4 squares?

13. On grid paper, show all the ways you can make a rectangle using the given number of squares. Find the perimeter of each rectangle.

a) 6 squares   b) 10 squares   c) 12 squares

ME5-13 Perimeter Problems

1. The picture shows a design for a garden. Find the perimeter of the garden by writing an addition equation.

a)
5 m
3 m   3 m
5 m

b)
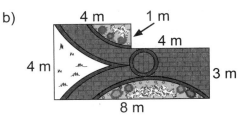
4 m   1 m
4 m
4 m   3 m
8 m

_____   _____

2. Each edge is 1 cm long. Write the total length of each side beside the figure (one side is done for you in part a). Then write an addition equation and find the perimeter.

a)

2 cm

Perimeter: _____

b)

Perimeter: _____

c)
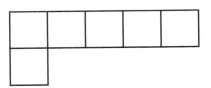

Perimeter: _____

d)
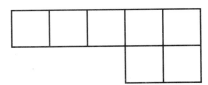

Perimeter: _____

3. Each edge is 1 unit long. Write the length of each side beside the figure (don't miss any edges!). Then use the side lengths to find the perimeter.

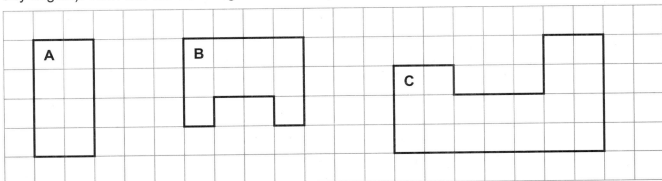

4. On grid paper, draw your own figures and find their perimeters. Try drawing letters or other shapes!

A rectangle has perimeter 12 m. Each side is an exact number of metres long. What are the dimensions of the rectangle? Let's try different widths. Try 1 m first.

The widths add to 2 m.
The missing lengths are 12 m − 2 m = 10 m altogether.
Each length is 10 m ÷ 2 = 5 m.

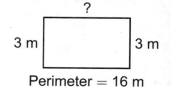

5. a) The widths add to _____ m.

   b) The missing lengths are 16 m − _____ m = _____ m altogether.

   c) Each length is _____ m ÷ 2 = _____ m.

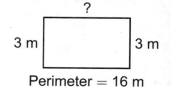

Perimeter = 16 m

6. a) The widths add to _____ m.

   b) The missing lengths are _____ altogether.

   c) Each length is _____ m.

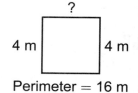

Perimeter = 16 m

7. Find the missing sides. (The pictures are not drawn to scale.)

   a) Perimeter = 24 m

   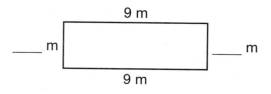

   b) Perimeter = 14 cm

   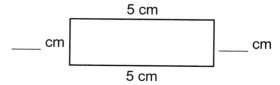

   c) Perimeter = 16 cm

   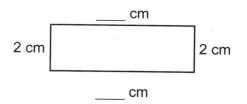

   BONUS ▶ Perimeter = 600 cm

   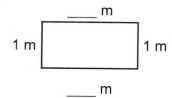

8. Find all rectangles with the given perimeter (with lengths and widths that are exact numbers of units).

   a) Perimeter = 8 units

Width	Length

   b) Perimeter = 12 units

Width	Length

   c) Perimeter = 14 units

Width	Length

   d) Perimeter = 18 units

Width	Length

BONUS ▶ Write a rule for finding the perimeter of a rectangle from its width and length.

9. a) About how many bicycles, parked end to end, would fit along the width of

   your classroom? _____

   b) A bicycle is about 2 m long. About how many metres wide is your classroom? _____

   c) About how many metres long is your classroom? _____

   d) What is the perimeter of your classroom? about _____

10. The length of a *square* room is about 3 bicycles. A bike is about 2 m long.

    a) About how many metres long is the room? _____

    b) What is the perimeter of the room? about _____

11. What unit (cm, m, or km) would you use to measure the perimeter of the object?

    a) a house _____   b) a book _____

    c) a schoolyard _____   d) a nature park _____

    e) a calculator _____   f) a city _____

    g) a basketball court _____   h) a country _____

12. Estimate the perimeter of a room in your home. Explain how you estimated the perimeter.

13. a) A square has sides 5 cm long. What is its perimeter?

    b) How could you find the perimeter of a square without drawing a picture?

    c) A square has perimeter 12 cm. How long is one side? Explain.

14. Sally arranged four squares (each with sides 1 m) to make a poster.
    She wants to make a border from ribbon for her poster.
    Ribbon costs 15¢ for each metre.

    How much will the border cost?

    ⊢1 m

15. How could you measure the perimeter of a round object (like a plate or a can)
    using a strip of paper and a ruler?

16. Can two different shapes have the same perimeter? Use grid paper to explain.

17. Emma says the rule "2 × (length + width)" gives the perimeter of a rectangle.
    Is she correct? Explain.

ME5-14 Area

The **area** of a flat shape is the amount of space it takes up.

A **square centimetre** (cm²) is a unit for measuring area.

A square with sides 1 cm has an area of 1 cm².

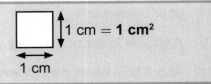

1 cm = **1 cm²**

1 cm

1. Find the area of the figure in square centimetres.

a)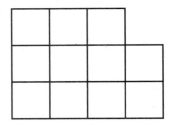

Area = _____ cm²

b)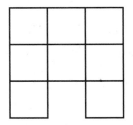

Area = _____ cm²

c)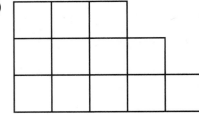

Area = _____ cm²

2. Using a ruler, draw lines to join the marks and divide the rectangle into square centimetres. Then find the area.

a)

Area = _____ cm²

b)

Area = _____ cm²

c)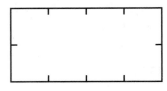

Area = _____ cm²

3. Find the area of the rectangles in square centimetres.

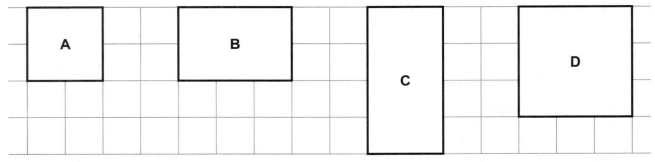

Area of A = _____ cm²   Area of B = _____ cm²   Area of C = _____ cm²   Area of D = _____ cm²

4. Use 1 cm grid paper.

a) Draw two different rectangles with an area of 10 cm².

b) Draw two figures that are not rectangles with an area of 10 cm².

c) Draw three different rectangles with an area of 16 cm². (Remember that a square is a rectangle too!)

d) Find the perimeter of the rectangles in part c). Which rectangle has the smallest perimeter?

A **square metre** (m²) is a unit for measuring area.

A square with sides 1 m has an area of 1 m².

For example, four unfolded pages from a newspaper are about 1 m².

1 m = **1 m²**

1 m

5. Jack measured the areas of objects at school, but he forgot to write down the units.
Fill in the blank with "m²" or "cm²."

a) The board measures 2 _____.

b) The notebook cover measures 310 _____.

c) The sticker measures 12 _____.

d) The classroom measures 75 _____.

6. Choose a unit of measure for the area. Estimate and then measure the area of the object.

	Object	Unit	Estimate	Actual Area
a)	classroom			
b)	board eraser			
c)	classroom door			
d)	computer monitor			
e)	sheet of paper			

7. a) Draw three different rectangles with a perimeter of 12 cm.

b) Find the area of the rectangles you drew in part a) and write them on the grid.

c) Which rectangle has the greatest area? _____

8. If 100 cm is equal to 1 m, is 100 cm² equal to 1 m²? Explain. _____

_____

BONUS ▶ How would you change a measurement in square metres to one in square centimetres?

_____

ME5-15 Area and Perimeter of Rectangles

1. Write a multiplication statement for the array.

a)

b)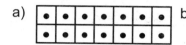

c)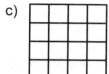

d)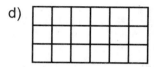

_____   _____   _____   _____

2. Draw a dot in each box. Then write a multiplication statement that tells you the number of boxes in the rectangle.

a)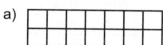

b)

c)

d)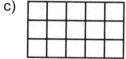

  ___2 × 7 = 14___   _____   _____   _____

3. Write the number of boxes along the length and the width of the rectangle.
Then write a multiplication equation for the area of the rectangle (in square units).

a)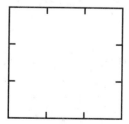

b)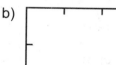

c)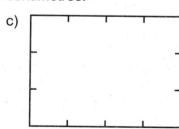

Width = _____   Width = _____   Width = _____

Length = _____   Length = _____   Length = _____

_____   _____   _____

4. Using a ruler, draw lines to join the marks and divide the rectangle into square centimetres.
Write a multiplication equation for the area of the rectangle in square centimetres.

a)

b)

c)

Area = _____   Area = _____   Area = _____

5. How can you find the area of a rectangle from its length and width?

_____

_____

6. Measure the length and width of the rectangle. Find the area. Include the units!

a)

_____

b)

_____

c)

_____

7. Area is also measured in other square units. Predict the name of the unit.

a)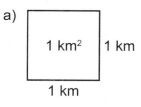

1 km² | 1 km

1 km

square kilometre

b)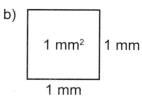

1 mm² | 1 mm

1 mm

_____

c)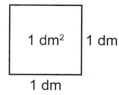

1 dm² | 1 dm

1 dm

_____

8. a) Calculate the area of each rectangle (include the units).

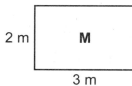

2 m | **M**

3 m

Area = _____

9 cm | **J**

6 cm

Area = _____

7 dm | **U**

6 dm

Area = _____

6 km | **P**

4 km

Area = _____

b) List the rectangles from least area to greatest area: _____, _____, _____, _____

What does it spell? _____

9. Find the area of the rectangle using the length and the width. Include the units!

a) Length = 7 m
Width = 5 m

Area = ___7 m × 5 m___

= ___35 m²___

b) Length = 9 m
Width = 2 m

Area = _____

= _____

c) Length = 8 cm
Width = 6 cm

Area = _____

= _____

d) Length = 7 dm
Width = 11 dm

Area = _____

= _____

e) Length = 9 mm
Width = 12 mm

Area = _____

= _____

f) Length = 12 km
Width = 3 km

Area = _____

= _____

10. a) The edge of each grid square represents 1 cm. For each shape, calculate the perimeter and area and write your answers in the chart below.

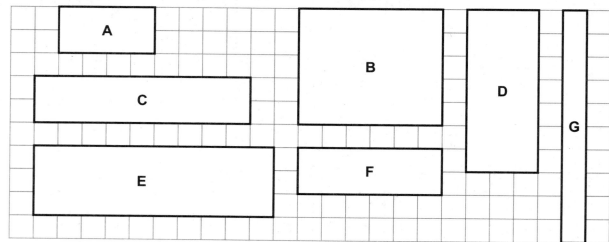

Shape	Perimeter	Area
A	$2 + 4 + 2 + 4 = 12$ cm	$2 \times 4 = 8$ cm²
B		
C		
D		
E		
F		
G		

b) Shape C has a greater perimeter than shape D. Does it also have a greater area? _____

c) Name two other shapes where one has a greater perimeter and the other a greater area: _____

d) Write the shapes in order from greatest to least perimeter: _____

e) Write the shapes in order from greatest to least area: _____

f) Are the orders in parts d) and e) the same? _____

g) What is similar about **perimeter** and **area**? What is different?

11. Ethan's lawn is 6 m wide and 9 m long.

a) Find the area of Ethan's lawn.

b) Pieces of sod are sold in 1 m by 2 m rectangular shapes. How many pieces of sod does Ethan need in order to cover the entire lawn?

c) Each 1 m by 2 m piece of sod costs $25. How much will it cost Ethan to cover the entire lawn with sod?

ME5-16 Problems with Area and Perimeter

Area of a rectangle = length × width   OR   Area = $\ell \times w$

1. Find the area of the rectangle.

   a) Width = 3 m
      Length = 6 m

      Area = _____

      = _____

   b) Width = 2 km
      Length = 9 km

      Area = _____

      = _____

   c) Width = 65 cm
      Length = 80 cm

      Area = _____

      = _____

   d) Width = 3 km
      Length = 66 km

      Area = _____

      = _____

   e) Width = 42 mm
      Length = 93 mm

      Area = _____

      = _____

   f) Width = 25 m
      Length = 140 m

      Area = _____

      = _____

2. Write an equation for the area of the rectangle. Then find the unknown width.

   a) Width = w cm
      Length = 5 cm
      Area = 15 cm²

      $w \times 5 = 15$

      $w = 15 \div 5$

      $w = 3$ cm

   b) Width = w m
      Length = 2 m
      Area = 12 m²

   c) Width = w km
      Length = 6 km
      Area = 24 km²

3. Write an equation for the area of the rectangle. Then find the unknown length.

   a) Width = 5 cm
      Length = ℓ cm
      Area = 30 cm²

   b) Width = 7 km
      Length = ℓ km
      Area = 63 km²

   BONUS ▶ Width = 10 m
      Length = ℓ m
      Area = 1678 m²

4. a) A rectangle has an area of 48 m² and a width of 3 m. What is its length?

   b) A rectangle has an area of 5600 cm² and a length of 80 cm. What is its width?

   c) A square has an area of 16 cm². What is its width?

5. Draw a line to divide the shape into two rectangles. Use the areas of the rectangles to find the total area of the shape.

a)

10 cm
4 cm
7 cm
6 cm
3 cm   4 cm

Area of rectangle 1 = _____

Area of rectangle 2 = _____

Total area = _____

b)

4 m   3 m
4 m
7 m
4 m
8 m

Area of rectangle 1 = _____

Area of rectangle 2 = _____

Total area = _____

c)

2 cm
5 cm
8 cm   7 cm
3 cm
9 cm

Area of rectangle 1 = _____

Area of rectangle 2 = _____

Total area = _____

d)

2 m
4 m
6 m
3 m

Area of rectangle 1 = _____

Area of rectangle 2 = _____

Total area = _____

REMINDER ▶ Perimeter is the distance around a shape.

---

6. Find the length and the area of the rectangle.

a) Width = 2 cm   Perimeter = 12 cm

Length = _____

Area = _____

b) Width = 4 cm   Perimeter = 20 cm

Length = _____

Area = _____

7. Ivan wants to build a rectangular vegetable garden 2 m wide and with a perimeter of 16 m.

a) Sketch the garden on grid paper. Each square on the grid represents one square metre.

b) What is the length of the vegetable garden?

c) Ivan wants to build a fence around the garden. Fencing costs $5 per metre. How much will the fencing cost?

d) Ivan will plant 8 cucumber seeds on each square metre of land. A pack of 50 seeds costs $2. How many packs of seeds does he need?

e) How much will the seeds and fencing cost altogether?

ME5-17 Stacking Blocks

1. How many blocks are in the shaded row?

a)

_____ blocks

b)

_____ blocks

c)

_____ blocks

2. How many blocks are in the shaded row?

a)

_____ blocks

b)

_____ blocks

c)

_____ blocks

3. Write the number of shaded blocks. Then write an addition equation and a multiplication equation for all the blocks.

a)

_____ blocks shaded

_____ + _____ + _____

= _____ blocks

_____ × _3_ = _____ blocks

b)

_____ blocks shaded

_____ + _____ + _____

= _____ blocks

_____ × _____ = _____ blocks

c)

_____ blocks shaded

_____ + _____ + _____ + _____

= _____ blocks

_____ × _____ = _____ blocks

4. a) Write a multiplication equation for the number of blocks in one layer.

_____ × _____ = _____ blocks

b) Calculate the number of blocks in the shaded layer. Then calculate the total number of blocks in the stack.

i)

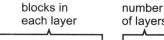

blocks in each layer   number of layers

_____ × _____ × _____

= _____ blocks

ii)

_____ × _____ × _____

= _____ blocks

iii)

_____ × _____ × _____

= _____ blocks

5. Write a multiplication statement for the number of blocks in the stack.

a)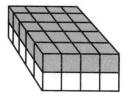

_____ × _____ × _____

= _____ blocks

b)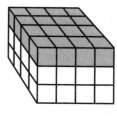

_____ × _____ × _____

= _____ blocks

c)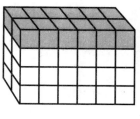

_____ × _____ × _____

= _____ blocks

6. a)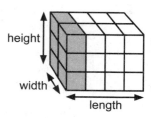

Number of blocks in a vertical layer

= height × width

= _3_ × _2_ = _6_ blocks

Total number of blocks

= height × width × length

= _____ × _____ × _____ = _____ blocks

b)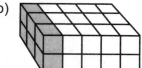

Number of blocks in a vertical layer

= height × width

= _____ × _____ = _____ blocks

Total number of blocks

= height × width × length

= _____ × _____ × _____ = _____ blocks

c)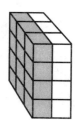

Number of blocks in a vertical layer

= height × width

= _____ × _____ = _____ blocks

Total number of blocks

= height × width × length

= _____ × _____ × _____ = _____ blocks

d)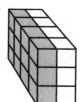

Number of blocks in a vertical layer

= height × width

= _____ × _____ = _____ blocks

Total number of blocks

= height × width × length

= _____ × _____ × _____ = _____ blocks

7. Three stacks in Question 6 have the same number of blocks. Use the height, width, length, and the properties of multiplication to explain why this happens.

ME5-18 Volume

> **Volume** is the amount of space taken up by a three-dimensional object.
> These objects have a volume of 4 cubes.

1. Count the number of cubes to find the volume of the object.

a)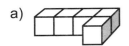

Volume = _____ cubes

b)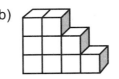

Volume = _____ cubes

c)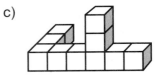

Volume = _____ cubes

> We measure volume in cubic units or unit cubes. (The cubes are not drawn to scale.)
>
> $1 \text{ cm}^3 = 1$ cubic centimetre $1 \text{ m}^3 = 1$ cubic metre $1 \text{ dm}^3 = 1$ cubic decimetre
>
> 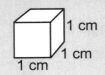 1 cm / 1 cm / 1 cm   1 m / 1 m / 1 m   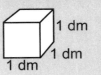 1 dm / 1 dm / 1 dm

---

2. Find the volume of the object made from unit cubes. Include units in your answer.

a) 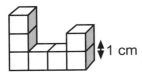 1 cm

Volume = _____

b) 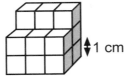 1 cm

Volume = _____

c) 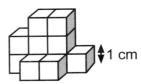 1 cm

Volume = _____

d) 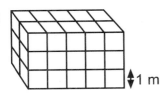 1 m

Volume = _____

e) 1 m

Volume = _____

f) 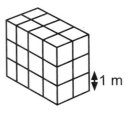 1 m

Volume = _____

g) 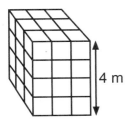 4 m

Volume = _____

h) 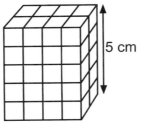 5 cm

Volume = _____

i) 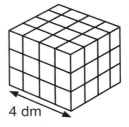 4 dm

Volume = _____

Mathematicians call rectangular boxes **rectangular prisms**.

3. Use two ways to find the volume of the rectangular prism made from unit cubes.

   a) Find the number of unit cubes. Include units in the answer.

   i)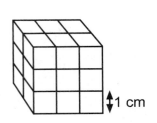

   Volume = _____

   ii)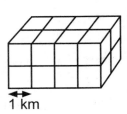

   Volume = _____

   iii)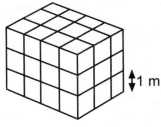

   Volume = _____

   b) Find the length, width, and height of the prisms in part a). Multiply length × width × height to find the volume. Include the units!

   i) Length = _____

   Width = _____

   Height = _____

   Volume = _____

   ii) Length = _____

   Width = _____

   Height = _____

   Volume = _____

   iii) Length = _____

   Width = _____

   Height = _____

   Volume = _____

   c) Compare your answers for volume in parts a) and b). Did you get the same answer both ways?

For a rectangular prism, volume = length × width × height   OR $V = \ell \times w \times h$.

4. Jun has a box that is 15 cm long, 10 cm wide, and 8 cm tall. He packs the box with 1 cm cubes.

   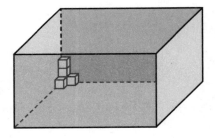

   a) How many cubes fit along each side of the box?

   Length = _____ cubes

   Width = _____ cubes

   Height = _____ cubes

   b) How many cubes does Jun need to fill the box? _____

   c) What is the volume of the box? _____ cubes = _____ cm³

   d) Use the formula volume = length × width × height to find the volume of the box.

   Volume = _____ cm × _____ cm × _____ cm = _____ cm³

   e) Did you get the same answer in parts c) and d)? If not, find your mistake.

5. Find the volume of the prism.

a) Length = __3 m__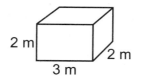

Width = __2 m__   2 m

Height = __2 m__   3 m   2 m

Volume = __3 m × 2 m × 2 m__ = __12 m³__

b) Length = _____    2 m

Width = _____   9 m

Height = _____   4 m

Volume = _____ = _____

c) Length = _____   2 cm

Width = _____   4 cm

Height = _____   5 cm

Volume = _____ = _____

d) Length = _____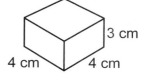

Width = _____   5 cm   5 cm

Height = _____   9 cm

Volume = _____ = _____

e) ℓ = _____

w = _____   6 dm

h = _____   6 dm   11 dm

V = _____ = _____

f) ℓ = _____

w = _____   3 cm

h = _____   4 cm   4 cm

V = _____ = _____

6. Find the volume of the rectangular prism with the given measurements.

a) Length 25 m, width 6 m, height 6 m

Volume = _____ = _____

b) Length 15 cm, width 30 cm, height 45 cm

Volume = _____ = _____

c) Length 90 cm, width 15 cm, height 8 cm

Volume = _____ = _____

d) Length 115 m, width 20 m, height 30 m

Volume = _____ = _____

7. Use this prism to explain why 2 × 3 × 4 = 3 × 2 × 4.

_____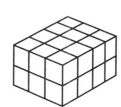

_____

_____

8. Estimate the answer. Then use a calculator to find the actual value.

a) First Canadian Place in Toronto, ON, is a rectangular prism that is 72 m wide, 68 m long, and 298 m tall. What is the volume of the tower?

b) The Cheung Kong Center Tower in Hong Kong, China, is a rectangular prism that is 47 m wide, 47 m long, and 283 m tall. What is the volume of the tower?

c) Which tower has a greater volume, the First Canadian Place or the Cheung Kong Center Tower? What is the difference between them?

ME5-19 Volume and Area of One Face

Flat surfaces on a three-dimensional (or 3-D) shape are called **faces**. Faces meet at **edges**. Edges meet at **vertices**. You can show hidden edges with dashed lines.

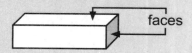 faces

hidden edges 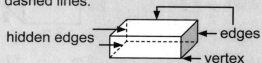 edges
vertex

1. Draw dashed lines to show the hidden edges. The dot marks a hidden vertex.

    a) 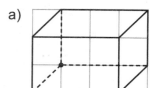   b) 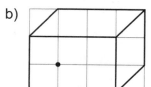   c) 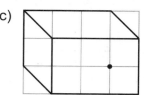   d)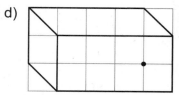

The edges and vertices of a shape make its **skeleton**. This is the skeleton of a cube.

2. Imagine the skeleton covered in paper and placed on a table. Trace the edges that would be hidden.

    a)    b) 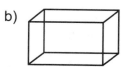   c)    d)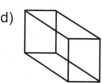

3. The top face and the bottom face are the **horizontal faces**. Shade the horizontal faces on the prism.

    a) 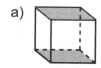   b) 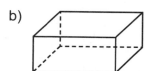   c)   d)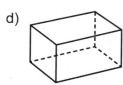

4. The bottom face of the rectangular prism has an area of 8 cm².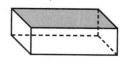

    What is the area of the shaded face? _____

5. a) What is the volume of the bottom layer of this prism? _____

    b) What is the volume of the top layer? _____

    c) Are the volumes of the bottom and the top layers the same? _____

    BONUS ▶

    d) What is the volume of the left layer? _____ Right layer? _____

    e) Are the volume of the left and the right layers the same? _____

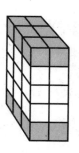

6. These prisms are made from 1 cm cubes.

   a) Fill in the table.

	i) height	ii)	iii)	iv)
Area of a Horizontal Face	6 cm²			
Volume of Shaded Layer	6 cm³			
Height of Prism	4 cm			
Number of Horizontal Layers	4			
Volume of Prism	24 cm³			

   b) What do you get if you multiply the volume of a shaded layer and the number of
      horizontal layers in the table above? _____

   c) Do you get the volume of the prism if you multiply the area of a horizontal face
      and the height of the prism in the table above? _____

7. Circle the part of the formula for the volume of a prism that shows the area of a
   horizontal face.

   Volume = length × width × height

> For a rectangular prism,
> Volume = length × width × height   OR   Volume = area of horizontal face × height.

8. Find the volume. Remember to include the units in your answer.

   a)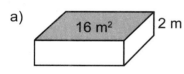

   Volume = _____ × _____

   = _____

   b)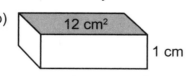

   Volume = _____ × _____

   = _____

   c)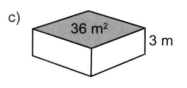

   Volume = _____ × _____

   = _____

   d) Area of top face = 12 m²
      Height = 10 m
      Volume = _____ × _____
      = _____

   e) Area of top face = 15 m²
      Height = 4 m
      Volume = _____ × _____
      = _____

   f) Area of top face = 22 cm²
      Height = 3 cm
      Volume = _____ × _____
      = _____

ME5-20 Liquid Volume

The volume of liquids is often measured in **litres** (L).
One litre is a little more than 4 cups.

1. Circle the objects that can hold more than 1 litre.

Small quantities of liquid are measured in **millilitres** (mL). One teaspoon holds 5 mL of liquid.

2. Circle the appropriate unit, litres (L) or millilitres (mL), to measure how much the container can hold.

   a)

   L   mL

   b)

   L   mL

   c)

   L   mL

   d)

   L   mL

3. Circle the best unit to measure how much the container can hold.

   a) a glass for water   b) a large pail   c) a sink   d) a small can of juice

   mL   L   mL   L   mL   L   mL   L

4. Circle the amount the container can likely hold.

   a) a large mug   b) an aquarium   c) a bathtub   d) a bottle of water

   500 mL   500 L   200 mL   200 L   300 mL   300 L   500 mL   500 L

1 litre = 1000 millilitres   1 L = 1000 mL

5. a) Fill in the table.

L	1	2	3	4	5	6	7	8
mL	1000							

   b) To change a measurement from litres (L) to millilitres (mL), what number do you

   multiply by? _____

6. Convert the measurement in litres to millilitres.

   a) 10 L = _____ mL   b) 13 L = _____ mL   c) 20 L = _____ mL

   d) 45 L = _____ mL   e) 72 L = _____ mL   f) 100 L = _____ mL

7. Convert the measurement in litres to millilitres. Then circle the greater measurement.

   a) 400 mL   3 L   b) 9300 mL   8 L   c) 2467 mL   23 L

             (3000 mL)

   d) 6666 mL   6 L   e) 70 L   7800 mL   f) 75 L   65 203 mL

8. a) Write a measurement in millilitres that is between 7 L and 8 L. _____

   b) Write a measurement in whole litres that is between 6905 mL and 7603 mL. _____

9. A container can hold the given volume of liquid. How many containers do you need to make a litre?

   a) 100 mL   b) 200 mL   c) 500 mL   d) 250 mL

   ___10___ containers   _____ containers   _____ containers   _____ containers

10. Jane bought: 2 L of juice   a 500 mL bottle of canola oil   a 1 L bottle of dish soap

   What is the total volume of liquid in millilitres that Jane bought? _____

11. a) A small aquarium holds the same amount of water as two 8 L pails. Write the amount of water that the aquarium can hold in litres and millilitres.

       _____ L or _____ mL

   b) A jar holds 500 mL of water. How many jars of water do you need to fill the aquarium? _____

12. A store has three different sizes of containers available.

   a) How many containers of size C do you need to hold 20 L of water total?

   b) How many containers of size A do you need to hold as much water as 4 containers of size B?

   c) Which holds more, 5 containers of size B or 3 containers of size C?

ME5-21 Litres and Millilitres

Carl multiplies by 1000 to convert 0.64 L to millilitres. First he writes the decimal as thousandths. Then he shifts the decimal point three places to the right: 0.64 L = 0.640 L = 640 mL.

1. Convert the measurement in litres to millilitres.

   a) 1.7 L = ___1.700___ L = ___1700___ mL   b) 0.59 L = _____ L = _____ mL

   c) 2.54 L = _____ L = _____ mL   d) 0.02 L = _____ L = _____ mL

   e) 0.004 L = _____ mL   f) 1.759 L = _____ mL

   g) 1.04 L = _____ mL   h) 24.7 L = _____ mL

2. Convert the measurement in litres to millilitres. Then circle the greater measurement.

   a) 500 mL   4 L   b) 3200 mL   3 L   c) 14 578 mL   17 L

   (4000 mL)

   d) 3400 mL   2.5 L   e) 4.6 L   4587 mL   f) 11.790 L   12 080 mL

   g) 6750 mL   6.95 L   h) 7.40 L   6800 mL   i) 3.047 L   350 mL

3. a) Write a measurement in millilitres that is between 5.39 L and 5.4 L. _____

   b) Write a measurement in litres that is between 3720 mL and 4017 mL. _____

4. Convert the measurement in litres to a mixed measurement.

   a) 6.79 L = ___6___ L ___790___ mL   b) 3.247 L = _____ L _____ mL

   c) 4.027 L = _____ L _____ mL   d) 5.82 L = _____ L _____ mL

   e) 5.008 L = _____ L _____ mL   f) 12.75 L = _____ L _____ mL

   g) 2.7 L = _____ L _____ mL   h) 58.1 L = _____ L _____ mL

5. Convert the measurement in millilitres to a mixed measurement.

   a) 5130 mL = ___5___ L ___130___ mL   b) 5217 mL = _____ L _____ mL

   c) 4367 mL = _____ L _____ mL   d) 4081 mL = _____ L _____ mL

   e) 7006 mL = _____ L _____ mL   f) 44 300 mL = _____ L _____ mL

6. A container can hold the given volume of liquid. How many containers are needed to make 3 L?

    a) 500 mL   b) 100 mL   c) 150 mL   d) 125 mL

7. Karen bought: 1.5 L of juice   a 400 mL bottle of canola oil   a 2.3 L bottle of soda

    a) What is the total volume of liquid in millilitres that Karen bought? _____

    BONUS ▶ What is the total volume in litres? _____

8. a) An aquarium can hold 160 L of water. How much water can the aquarium

       hold in millilitres? _____

    b) A pail holds 8 L of water. How many pails do you need to fill the aquarium?

    c) How many 2 L water bottles do you need to fill the aquarium?

    d) If you fill the aquarium completely, can you put any fish in it? _____

9. Fred makes juice from concentrate by mixing a 333 mL can of concentrate with three cans of water. How much juice does he make?

10. Orange juice comes in boxes of 125 mL and 200 mL. A pack of six boxes, each 200 mL, costs $7 per pack. A pack of eight boxes, each 125 mL, costs $6 per pack.

    a) How much juice is in each pack? Write your answer in millilitres.

    b) Which contains more juice, five packs of six juice boxes or six packs of eight juice boxes?

    c) Which costs more, five packs of six boxes or six packs of eight juice boxes?

    d) Which way of buying the juice is cheaper by volume? Explain. _____

_____

ME5-22 Filling Containers

> **Capacity** is the amount of liquid (or rice, beans, and so on) that a container can hold.
>
> A container with a volume of 1 cubic centimetre (1 cm³) has a capacity of 1 millilitre (1 mL).

1. a) What is the volume of a cube with sides 1 dm = 10 cm?

    Volume = 1 dm³ = _____ cm × _____ cm × _____ cm = _____ cm³

    b) How many cubic centimetres are in 1 dm³? _____

    c) How many millilitres are in 1 L? _____

> A container with a volume of 1 cubic decimetre (1 dm³) has a capacity of 1 litre (1 L).

2. Find the capacity of the container and the volume of liquid in it.

    a)

    Capacity = _____ L

    Volume = _____ L

    b)

    Capacity = _____ L

    Volume = _____ L

    c)

    Capacity = _____ L

    Volume = _____ L

3. a) A can has a volume of 3 dm³. What is its capacity in litres? _____

    b) A jar has a volume of 750 cm³. What is its capacity in millilitres? _____

    c) A can has a capacity of 355 mL. What is its volume in cubic centimetres? _____

    d) A juice container has a capacity of 2.63 L. What is its volume? _____

4. Find the volume and the capacity of the aquarium. Include the units!

    a)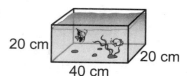

    Length = ___40 cm___

    Width = ___20 cm___

    Height = ___20 cm___

    Volume = ___40 cm × 20 cm × 20 cm___

          = ___16 000 cm³___

    Capacity = ___16 000 mL___

    b)

    Length = _____

    Width = _____

    Height = _____

    Volume = _____

          = _____

    Capacity = _____

5. Use two ways to find the capacity of the prism.

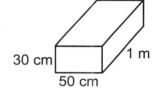

a) Find the volume in cubic centimetres. Then convert cm³ to mL.

Volume = _____ cm³, so capacity = _____ mL.

b) Convert the measurements to decimetres.

Length = _____ dm   Width = _____ dm   Height = _____ dm

c) Find the volume in cubic decimetres. Then convert dm³ to litres.

Volume = _____ dm³, so capacity = _____ L.

d) How should your answers in parts a) and c) be related? Explain.
Are they related this way? If not, find your mistake.

_____

_____

6. Find the capacity of the prism.

a) Convert all the measurements to centimetres.

Length = _____ cm   Width = _____ cm   Height = _____ cm

b) Find the volume in cubic centimetres. Then convert cm³ to mL.

Volume = _____ cm³, so capacity = _____ mL.

c) What is the capacity of the prism in litres? _____ L

7. An aquarium has a length of 40 cm and a width of 25 cm. The water in the aquarium
is 10 cm high. How much water is in the aquarium?

_____ mL = _____ L

BONUS ▶ Find the volume of the prism. Then find the height.
Hint: use Volume = area of horizontal face × height.

a) Capacity = 36 mL

Volume = _____

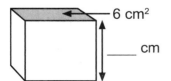

b) Capacity = 320 L

Volume = _____

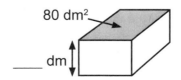

c) Capacity = 90 mL

Volume = _____

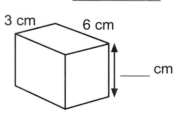

ME5-23 Mass Review

> **Mass** is the amount of matter in an object. The heavier an object, the greater its mass.
> The mass of small objects is often measured in **grams** (g).
>
> A large paper clip and a chocolate chip each weigh about 1 gram.

1. The mass of a quarter is about 5 g.

    a) What is the mass of 10 quarters? _____   50 quarters? _____

    b) What is the mass of the amount in quarters?

    i) 25¢ _____   ii) 50¢ _____   iii) 125¢ _____   iv) 200¢ _____

> Mass is also measured in **kilograms** (kg).
>
> A tall, thin carton of orange juice has a mass of about 1 kg.

2. Estimate and circle the correct mass for the item.

    a)   b)    c)    d)

    100 g   100 kg   20 g   20 kg   35 g   35 kg   4 g   4 kg

> 1 kilogram = 1000 grams   1 kg = 1000 g

3. Fill in the table.

kg	1	2	3	4	5	6	7	8
g	1000							

4. a) To convert a measurement in kilograms to grams, I multiply by _____.

    b) Change the measurement to grams.

    i) 13 kg = _____   ii) 49 kg = _____   iii) 107 kg = _____

5. Convert the measurement in kilograms to grams. Then circle the greater measurement.

    a) 500 g (7 kg)   b) 9300 g   91 kg   c) 34 768 g   15 kg

        7000 g

    d) 2222 g   2 kg   e) 70 kg   7320 g   f) 47 kg   46 203 g

Alice multiplies by 1000 to convert 0.32 kg to grams. She writes the decimal as thousandths.
Then she shifts the decimal point three places to the right: 0.32 kg = 0.320 kg = 320 g.

6. Convert the measurement in kilograms to grams.

    a) 1.6 kg = ___1.600___ kg = _____ g   b) 0.89 kg = _____ kg = _____ g

    c) 2.83 kg = _____ kg = _____ g   d) 0.02 kg = _____ kg = _____ g

    e) 0.004 kg = _____ g   f) 1.789 kg = _____ g

    g) 1.03 kg = _____ g   h) 23.6 kg = _____ g

7. Convert the measurement in kilograms to a mixed measurement.

    a) 6.79 kg = ___6___ kg ___790___ g   b) 3.247 kg = _____ kg _____ g

    c) 4.027 kg = _____ kg _____ g   d) 5.82 kg = _____ kg _____ g

    e) 2.7 kg = _____ kg _____ g   f) 58.1 kg = _____ kg _____ g

8. Convert the measurement in grams to a mixed measurement.

    a) 5130 g = ___5___ kg ___130___ g   b) 7412 g = _____ kg _____ g

    c) 6274 g = _____ kg _____ g   d) 8081 g = _____ kg _____ g

    e) 9008 g = _____ kg _____ g   f) 57 400 g = _____ kg _____ g

9. Convert the mixed measurement to a measurement in grams.

    a) 3 kg = ___3000___ g   b) 5 kg = _____ g   c) 7 kg = _____ g

        so 3 kg 71 g   so 5 kg 630 g   so 7 kg 23 g

	3	0	0	0	g
+			7	1	g
=	3	0	7	1	g

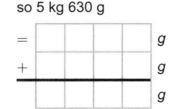

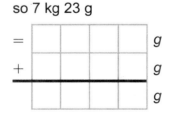

    d) 9 kg 128 g = _____ g   e) 12 kg 237 g = _____ g   f) 44 kg 3 g = _____ g

10. A mail carrier is carrying 300 letters in his bag. Each letter weighs about 20 g.
What is the total mass of the letters in kilograms?

11. a) Baby Mary weighs 3617 grams. Baby Josh weighs 4 kg. Who is heavier? Explain.

     b) Jennifer weighed 3.5 kg at birth. She grew at a rate of 200 g each week.
How much did Jennifer weigh when she was four weeks old?

ME5-24 Units of Mass

REMINDER ▶ 1 kilogram = 1000 grams	1 kg = 1000 g

1. Raj thinks that 2 kg is lighter than 15 g because 2 is less than 15. Is he correct? Explain.

   _____

2. a) Write a measurement in grams that is between 4.35 kg and 4.36 kg. _____

   b) Write a measurement in kilograms that is between 2674 g and 3196 g. _____

3. Convert the measurement in grams to a mixed measurement.

   a) 1530 g = ___1___ kg ___530___ g   b) 2639 g = _____ kg _____ g

   c) 5704 g = _____ kg _____ g   d) 3410 g = _____ kg _____ g

   e) 6019 g = _____ kg _____ g   f) 4007 g = _____ kg _____ g

---

We measure the mass of very small objects in **milligrams**. Write 1 **mg** for 1 milligram.

Here are some examples of masses in milligrams:

small ant: about 1 mg   sesame seed: about 4 mg   grain of rice: about 29 mg

---

4. Will you use grams or milligrams to measure the mass?

   a) grain of sand   b) dime   c) raindrop

      mg   g   mg   g   mg   g

We use milligrams when we need to be precise. For example, doctors use milligrams for medications.

---

5. Circle the measurement that fills the blank best.

   a) Each tablet contains _____ of vitamin C.   500 mg   500 g

   b) A dollar coin weighs about _____.   6 mg   6 g

   c) A jar can hold _____ of salt.   500 mg   500 g

   d) A table tennis ball weighs about _____.   3 mg   3 g

   BONUS ▶ A grain of sugar weighs about _____.   0.6 mg   0.6 kg

6. The cost of shipping a package is $4 per kilogram. How much does it cost to ship a package that weighs 12 kg?

We measure mass of very large objects in **tonnes**. Write 1 **t** for 1 tonne. 1 tonne = 1000 kg

Here are some examples of masses in tonnes:

small car: about 1 t   school bus: about 14 t   adult blue whale: about 140 t

7. Convert the measurement in tonnes into kilograms.

   a) 5 t = _____ kg   b) 18 t = _____ kg   c) 6 t = _____ kg   d) 50 t = _____ kg

   e) 1.5 t = _____ kg   f) 7.3 t = _____ kg   g) 4.55 t = _____ kg   h) 0.26 t = _____ kg

8. Choose the most appropriate unit (mg, g, kg, or t) to measure the mass of the object.

   a) elephant _____   b) spider _____   c) building _____   d) bag of rice _____

   e) envelope _____   f) polar bear _____   g) stapler _____   h) diamond _____

9. An average eleven-year-old child weighs about 40 kg, and an average adult weighs
    about 75 kg. Three adults plan to take 21 eleven-year-olds on a river rafting trip.
    The raft can carry 1 tonne. Can all the people ride on the raft?

10. a) An African elephant has a mass of about 5000 kg. How many tonnes is that?

    b) Elephants eat about 150 kg of food per day. Would an elephant eat more
        or less than 1 tonne in a week?

11. An empty bus weighs 10.5 t and can hold 40 passengers. Each passenger weighs
    70 kg on average.

    a) What is the weight of the empty bus in kilograms? _____

    b) What is the weight of 40 passengers? _____

    c) Each passenger can carry a bag that weighs up to 25 kg. What is the maximum
        weight of the bags for 40 passengers? _____

    BONUS ▶ A bus is full, with 40 passengers, a driver, and a tour guide. Each person
             on the bus has a bag weighing 25 kg. Can the bus go on a bridge that
             allows only vehicles that weigh 15 t or less? Explain.

PDM5-9 Outcomes

Any time you do something where different results are possible, you are doing an **experiment**.

When you flip a coin, the result is one of two possible **outcomes.**

When Alice plays tic-tac-toe with a friend, the result will be one of three possible outcomes:

    1. Alice wins.

    2. Alice loses.

    3. Nobody wins or loses.

1. List all the outcomes (possible results) of spinning the spinner in the table. How many outcomes are there in total?

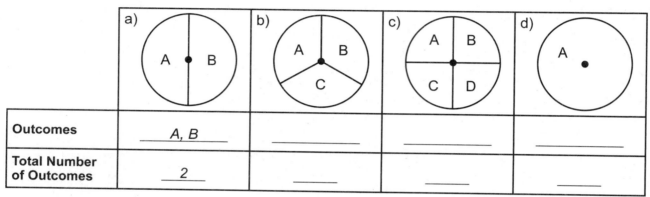

	a)	b)	c)	d)
Outcomes	_A, B_	_____	_____	_____
Total Number of Outcomes	_2_	_____	_____	_____

2. What are the possible outcomes when you flip a coin? ___*heads*___ , _____

3. Fill in the table.

		Outcomes	Total Number of Outcomes
a)	**A Chess Game**	*white wins,*	
b)	**Rolling a Six-Sided Die**		
c)	**A Baseball Game**		

4. You take one ball out of the box. List the outcomes. How many outcomes are there?

a)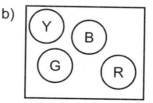

outcomes: _Y, R, B_

_3_ outcomes

b)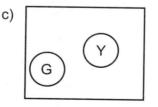

outcomes: _____

_____ outcomes

c)

outcomes: _____

_____ outcomes

d)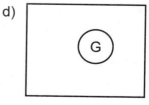

outcomes: _____

_____ outcome

Probability and Data Management 5-9

5. List all the outcomes and write the number of outcomes.

   a) spinning an even number: __2, 4, 6, 8__ , number of outcomes: __4__

   b) spinning an odd number: _____ , number of outcomes: _____

   c) spinning a number greater than 4: _____ , number of outcomes: _____

6. Ivan rolls a six-sided die. List all the outcomes and write the number of outcomes.

   a) rolling an even number: __2, 4, 6__ , number of outcomes: __3__

   b) rolling an odd number: _____ , number of outcomes: _____

   c) rolling a number greater than 4: _____ , number of outcomes: _____

7. List all the outcomes and write the number of outcomes.

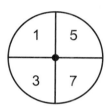

   spinning an odd number: _____ , number of outcomes: _____

   BONUS ▶ spinning an even number: _____ , number of outcomes: _____

Spinning the spinner on the right has four outcomes:

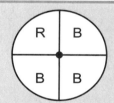

   1. The pointer lands in the top right. (B)
   2. The pointer lands in the bottom right. (B)
   3. The pointer lands in the bottom left. (B)
   4. The pointer lands in the top left. (R)

---

8. How many outcomes are there in total? How many red outcomes are there?

   a)
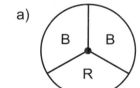
   _____ outcomes

   _____ red outcome

   b)
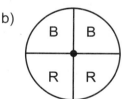
   _____ outcomes

   _____ red outcomes

   c)
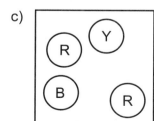
   _____ outcomes

   _____ red outcomes

   d)
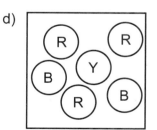
   _____ outcomes

   _____ red outcomes

   e)
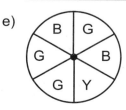
   _____ outcomes

   _____ red outcomes

   f)
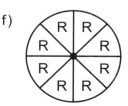
   _____ outcomes

   _____ red outcomes

PDM5-10 Even Chances

1. Shade half of the parts and fill in the blanks.

   a)

   _____ parts in half of a pie

   _____ parts in a pie

   b)

   _____ parts in half of a pie

   _____ parts in a pie

   c)

   _____ parts in half of a box

   _____ parts in a box

   d)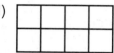

   _____ parts in half of a box

   _____ parts in a box

2. Circle half of the triangles.

   a)

   b)

   c)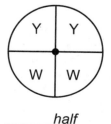

   d)

3. Divide by 2.

   a) $4 \div 2 =$ _____   b) $6 \div 2 =$ _____   c) $10 \div 2 =$ _____   d) $8 \div 2 =$ _____

4. Is the first number "more than half," "half," or "less than half" of the second number?
   Hint: Find half of the second number first.

   a) 4 is _____ *more than half* _____ of 6.

   b) 4 is _____ of 10.

   c) 5 is _____ of 10.

   d) 6 is _____ of 10.

   e) 6 is _____ of 14.

   f) 7 is _____ of 12.

   g) 9 is _____ of 18.

   h) 8 is _____ of 14.

5. Are more than half, half, or less than half of the regions white?

   a)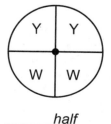

   _____ *half* _____

   b)

   _____

   c)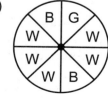

   _____

   d)

   _____

6. How many parts of the spinner are shaded? How many parts are there in total?
   Circle the spinner if exactly half of the spinner is shaded.

a)

_____ parts shaded

_____ parts in total

b)

_____ parts shaded

_____ parts in total

c)

_____ parts shaded

_____ parts in total

Half of the spinner is green. You expect to spin green half of the time.

There is an **even chance** of spinning green.

It is **equally likely** that you will spin green or blue.

| G | G |
| B | B |

7. Circle the spinners with an even chance of spinning green.

8. Six marbles are in a box. Three of them are yellow and the rest are red.

   a) Are exactly half of the marbles yellow? _____

   b) Is there an even chance of taking out a yellow marble? _____

   c) Is taking out a yellow marble or a red marble equally likely? _____

9. There are 14 marbles in a box. Six are green, four are red, and the rest are blue.

   a) Are exactly half of the marbles green? _____

   b) Is there an even chance of taking out a green marble? _____

   BONUS ▶ Is taking out a red marble or a blue marble equally likely? _____

        Explain. _____

10. a) A baseball team usually wins 5 out of 8 games. Does the team have an even

       chance of winning? _____

    b) A hockey team played 18 games and won 8 of them. Did the team win more than

       half of the games? _____ Explain. _____

    BONUS ▶ A basketball team played 13 games and won 7 of them. Did the team win

         more than half of the games? _____ Explain. _____

PDM5-11 Describing Probability

When you describe the result of spinning a spinner, rolling a die, or playing a game, you describe an **event**.

You expect an event with an **even chance** to happen exactly half of the time.
You expect a **likely** event to happen more than half of the time.
You expect an **unlikely** event to happen less than half of the time.

You will likely spin red on the spinner in the picture. You are unlikely to spin blue.

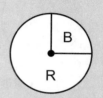

1. Describe the event as likely, unlikely, or having an even chance.

a)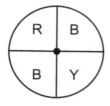

spinning red

unlikely

b)

spinning red

c)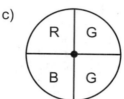

spinning green

d)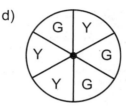

spinning green

2. Use "likely," "even chance," or "unlikely" to describe the event.

a)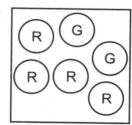

drawing red

b)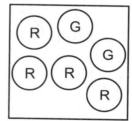

drawing green

c)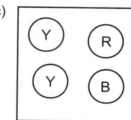

drawing yellow

d)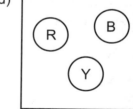

drawing red

3. Describe the chances of the event as unlikely, even, or likely.

a) 8 marbles in a box, 4 red marbles
   Event: You take out a red marble.

b) 10 marbles in a box, 6 red marbles
   Event: You take out a red marble.

c) 6 socks in a drawer, 4 black socks
   Event: You pull out a black sock.

d) 12 coins in a pocket, 3 dimes
   Event: You take out a dime.

e) You roll a die and get a 5 or 6.

BONUS ▶ 150 mm of rain will fall today.

4. What colour marble are you more likely to draw, red or blue? _____

Explain. _____

_____

If an event cannot happen, it is **impossible**. Rolling a 7 on a die is impossible since a die only has 1 to 6 on its faces.

If an event must happen, it is **certain**. When you toss a coin, it is certain that it will show heads or tails.

---

5. Use "certain," "likely," "even chance," "unlikely," or "impossible" to describe the event.

a)

spinning green

_____

b)

picking blue

_____

c)

picking green

_____

d)

picking green

_____

e)

spinning yellow

_____

f)

spinning red

_____

6. Fill in the blank with "less likely than," "more likely than," or "equally as likely as."
Hint: Count the number of marbles of each colour.

a) Drawing a red marble is _____ drawing a green marble.

b) Drawing a yellow marble is _____ drawing a red marble.

c) Drawing a blue marble is _____ drawing a green marble.

d) Drawing a white marble is _____ drawing a blue marble.

7. a) Design a spinner with red and blue parts where spinning red is less likely than spinning blue.

b) Design a spinner with red, blue, and green parts where spinning green is more likely than spinning blue.

c) Design a spinner with at least three parts where spinning green is impossible.

PDM5-12 Probability

The spinner has 4 equal sections and 3 of them are red.

So the **probability** that the spinner will land on red is $\frac{3}{4}$.

The fraction $\frac{3}{4}$ represents the number of ways to spin red (3, the numerator) out of the total number of outcomes (4, the denominator).

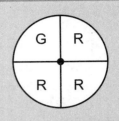

1. Fill in the blanks. What is the probability of spinning red?

a)    __2__ ways to spin red

                         __3__ equal sections in total

     The probability of spinning red is $\boxed{\dfrac{2}{3}}$.

b)    _____ ways to spin red

                         _____ equal sections in total

     The probability of spinning red is $\boxed{}$.

c) 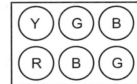   _____ way to spin red

                         _____ equal sections in total

     The probability of spinning red is $\boxed{}$.

d) 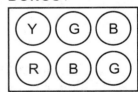   _____ way to spin red

                         _____ equal sections in total

     The probability of spinning red is $\boxed{}$.

2. Find the probability of picking a marble of the given colour.

a)

B	G
R	R

red: $\boxed{\dfrac{2}{4}}$

b)

B	G
R	R

green: $\boxed{}$

c)

Y	G	B
R	B	G

blue: $\boxed{}$

BONUS ▶

Y	G	B
R	B	G

not blue: $\boxed{}$

3. The six outcomes from rolling a regular die are: 1, 2, 3, 4, 5, or 6. Complete the table.
   Use equivalent fractions to write the probability as a fraction with the smallest numbers possible.

	Event	Outcomes that Make Up the Event	Probability of Event
a)	Rolling an even number	2, 4, 6	$\frac{3}{6} = \frac{1}{2}$
b)	Rolling a number greater than 4		
c)	Rolling a number less than 4		

                                        Probability and Data Management 5-12

4. Kim has 8 marbles in a box. She takes out a marble without looking. Fill in the table. Write the probability as a fraction with the smallest numbers possible.

(W) (W) (W) (W) (R) (R) (R) (B)

	Event	Number of Outcomes	Probability
a)	Pulling out a red marble		
b)	Pulling out a marble that is not red		
c)	Not pulling out a blue marble		
BONUS ▶	Pulling out a marble that is either white or red		

5. When Zack spins the spinner, he says the probability of spinning white is $\frac{1}{3}$ because it is 1 out of 3 possible outcomes. Explain his mistake.

R | B
W

_____

_____

BONUS ▶ What is the probability of spinning white? ☐

6. Write a fraction that gives the probability of spinning the given number.

a) the number 3 ☐

b) the number 1 ☐

1 | 3
7 | 1
6 | 5
9 | 4

c) an even number ☐

d) an odd number ☐

e) a number less than 5 ☐

f) a number greater than 5 ☐

7. Write a fraction that gives the probability of spinning the given letter.

a) the letter E ☐

b) the letter A ☐

c) a vowel ☐

A | E
C | T
A

d) a consonant ☐

e) a letter that appears in the word "Canada" ☐

8. Design a spinner with red and blue sections where the probability of spinning red is $\frac{5}{6}$.

PDM5-13 Expectations

The spinner has two outcomes. There is an equal chance of spinning grey or white.

We expect to spin grey $\frac{1}{2}$ of the time.

grey   white

We expect to spin white $\frac{1}{2}$ of the time.

If we spin the spinner 20 times, we expect to spin grey 10 times because 10 is half of 20.

1. a) If you flip a coin repeatedly, what fraction of the time would you expect it to land on each side?

   heads [ ]   tails [ ]

   b) Is there an equal chance of getting heads or tails? _____

2. a) Use division to find the answer.

   i) $\frac{1}{2}$ of 10 = ___10 ÷ 2 = 5___   ii) $\frac{1}{2}$ of 20 = _____

   iii) $\frac{1}{2}$ of 16 = _____   iv) $\frac{1}{2}$ of 48 = _____

   b) Complete the sentence: To find $\frac{1}{2}$ of a number, you can divide the number by _____.

   c) Complete the sentence: To find $\frac{1}{4}$ of a number, you can divide the number by _____.

3. Suppose you flip a coin 100 times.

   a) How many times do you expect it to land with heads facing up? _____

   b) How many times do you expect it to land with tails facing up? _____

There are four outcomes for this spinner: one is for grey and three are for white.

We expect to spin grey $\frac{1}{4}$ of the time.

grey   white
white   white

We expect to spin white $\frac{3}{4}$ of the time.

4. a) How many times do you expect grey when you spin the spinner …

   i) 4 times? ___1___   ii) 8 times? _____   iii) 12 times? _____

   iv) 16 times? _____   v) 20 times? _____   vi) 24 times? _____

   b) How many times do you expect white when you spin the spinner …

   i) 4 times? ___3___   ii) 8 times? _____   iii) 12 times? _____

   iv) 16 times? _____   v) 20 times? _____   vi) 24 times? _____

There are six outcomes when you roll a die. Four outcomes are less than 5: 1, 2, 3, and 4.
Two outcomes are greater than or equal to 5: 5 and 6.

We expect to roll a
number less than 5
$\frac{4}{6}$ of the time.

We expect to roll a number
greater than or equal to 5
$\frac{2}{6}$ of the time.

5. a) How many times do you expect to get a number less than 5 when you roll a die …

   i) 6 times? __4__   ii) 12 times? _____   iii) 18 times? _____

   b) How many times do you expect to get a number greater than or equal to 5 when you roll a die …

   i) 6 times? __2__   ii) 12 times? _____   iii) 18 times? _____

BONUS ▶ Shade any four of the numbers so that $\frac{4}{6}$ are shaded and $\frac{2}{6}$ are not shaded.

   a) How many times do you expect to get a shaded number when you roll a die …

   i) 6 times? _____   ii) 12 times? _____   iii) 18 times? _____

   b) How many times do you expect to get an unshaded number when you roll a die …

   i) 6 times? _____   ii) 12 times? _____   iii) 18 times? _____

6. a) Fill in the table.

	i)	ii)	iii)	BONUS ▶
Total Number of Outcomes	4			
Number of Grey Outcomes	3			
Number of White Outcomes	1			
Fraction of Grey Outcomes	$\frac{3}{4}$			
Fraction of White Outcomes	$\frac{1}{4}$			

   b) Simon spins each spinner in part a), i) to iii), 12 times. How many times does he
   expect it to land on each colour?

   i) grey __9__ white __3__   ii) grey _____ white _____   iii) grey _____ white _____

PDM5-14 Experiments in Probability

1. a) If you flip a coin repeatedly, what fraction of the time would you expect to get the result?

   i) heads [ ]

   ii) tails [ ]

   b) If you flip a coin 40 times, how many times would you expect to get the result?

   i) heads _____

   ii) tails _____

   c) Flip a coin 40 times and record the results in the tally chart.

Outcome	Prediction	Tally	Count
heads			
tails			

   d) Did the results match your expectations? Explain.

   _____

   _____

2. Which of the three results from 100 coin flips is most likely?

   A. 100 heads, 0 tails   **B.** 6 heads, 94 tails   **C.** 51 heads, 49 tails

   Explain. _____

> **REMINDER ▶** To find $\frac{1}{3}$ of a number, divide the number by 3. $\frac{1}{3}$ of $12 = 12 \div 3 = 4$.

3. a) If you spin the spinner 30 times, how many times would you expect to spin the colour?

   i) grey _____   ii) white _____

   b) Use a paper clip and pencil as a spinner. Spin 30 times. Record the results.

Outcome	Tally	Count
grey		
white		

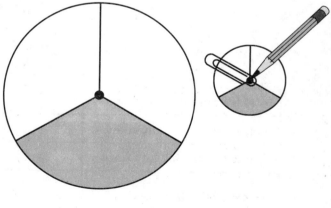

   c) Did your results match your expectations? Explain. _____

   _____

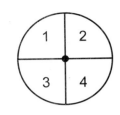

4. Jin and Cathy play a game with the spinner on the right. For each turn, the player spins twice and adds the numbers.

   a) Complete the table below to determine how many ways there are of getting the sum.

   i) 2: __1__ way   ii) 3: _____ ways   iii) 4: _____ ways   iv) 5: _____ ways

   v) 6: _____ ways   vi) 7: _____ ways   vii) 8: _____ way

Outcome of First Spin	Outcomes of Second Spin	Outcomes of Sums	Outcome of First Spin	Outcomes of Second Spin	Outcomes of Sums
1	1	_1_ + _1_ = _2_	2	1	_2_ + _1_ = _3_
	2	_1_ + _2_ = _3_		2	___ + ___ = ___
	3	___ + ___ = ___		3	___ + ___ = ___
	4	___ + ___ = ___		4	___ + ___ = ___
3	1	___ + ___ = ___	4	1	___ + ___ = ___
	2	___ + ___ = ___		2	___ + ___ = ___
	3	___ + ___ = ___		3	___ + ___ = ___
	4	___ + ___ = ___		4	___ + ___ = ___

   b) Which outcomes of sums have an equal chance of occurring? _____

   c) Which outcome of sums has the greatest chance of occurring? _____

   d) Take 32 turns spinning Jin and Cathy's spinner. For each turn, spin the spinner twice and add the outcomes. Record the results in the tally chart.

Sum	Tally	Count
2		
3		
4		
5		
6		
7		
8		

   e) Did your results match your expectations? Explain.

5. Amy wins if the coin lands on heads. Ben wins if it lands on tails. They flip the coin 24 times altogether and record the results in a tally chart. Amy says something is wrong because there has to be 12 heads and 12 tails. Do you agree? Explain.

H	JHT JHT I
T	JHT JHT III

PDM5-15 Games and Probability

In a **fair game**, all players have the same probability of winning.

1. Player A wins if the spinner lands on grey; Player B wins if the spinner lands on white. Circle the spinners that make the game fair.

2. Jack, Lynn, and Shelly have 10 cards with numbers 1 to 10. They pull a card without looking. Each player scores points depending on the number on the card:

   • Jack scores a point if the number is an odd number.

   • Lynn scores a point if the number is a 1, 2, 5, or 10.

   • Shelly scores a point if the number is a 3, 6, 9, or 10.

   a) What is the probability of each player scoring a point?

   Jack: [ ]   Lynn: [ ]   Shelly: [ ]

   b) Is the game fair? _____ Explain. _____

   _____

   c) How many points do you expect each player to score after 20 rounds? Circle the expected winner.

   Jack: _____   Lynn: _____   Shelly: _____

   d) Jack, Lynn, and Shelly pull a card 20 times. Here is the tally of the results.

Number on Card	1	2	3	4	5	6	7	8	9	10
Tally for Cards Drawn	|||	|||		|||	||			||			|||	||

   How much did each person score? Circle the winner.

   Jack: _____   Lynn: _____   Shelly: _____

   e) Is the winner the same as predicted in part c)? Explain.

   _____

   _____

3. Design a spinner with four parts where the result is fair for Player 1, Player 2, and Player 3.

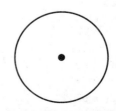

4. Mandy and Luc play a game of chance with the spinner shown. If it lands on yellow, Mandy wins. If it lands on red, Luc wins.

a) Luc and Mandy play the game 32 times. Predict how many times the spinner will land on red. _____

b) Use a paper clip and pencil as a spinner. Spin it 32 times and record the results in the tally chart and on the bar graph.

Outcome	Tally	Count
red		
green		
yellow		

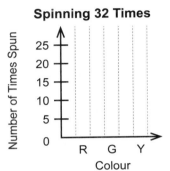

Were the results as you expected? _____

5. Write numbers on the spinner for the given probability.

a)

The probability of spinning a 3 is $\frac{1}{4}$.

b)

The probability of spinning an even number is $\frac{5}{6}$.

c)

The probability of spinning 3 or 6 is $\frac{2}{5}$.

BONUS ▶
The probability of spinning a 2 is $\frac{1}{3}$.

6. If you flip a coin 20 times, which tally chart would you be most likely to get? _____

A.	
Heads	Tails
卌 卌 卌	卌

B.	
Heads	Tails
卌 卌 丨	卌 丨丨丨丨

C.	
Heads	Tails
卌 丨丨	卌 卌 丨丨丨

Explain your choice. _____

_____

_____